Facilitator's Manual

On Course, Fourth Edition
Strategies for Creating Success in College and in Life

Skip Downing

HOUGHTON MIFFLIN COMPANY   Boston   New York

Senior Sponsoring Editor: Mary Finch
Developmental Editor: Shani B. Fisher
Editorial Assistants: Andrew Sylvester, Allison Seymour
Senior Manufacturing Coordinator: Priscilla Bailey
Marketing Manager: Barbara Lebuhn

Printed in the U.S.A.

ISBN: 0-618-37978-9

456789-QWF-09 08 07 06 05

Contents

Introduction

Purpose of This Book

On Course offers students the opportunity to learn essential skills for creating success in college and in life. At the center of the success skills addressed in *On Course* is the students' ability to make wise choices. *On Course* approaches the college experience as a laboratory where students practice making wise choices that support not only their academic success but their personal and professional success as well.

Teaching college students how to make wise choices is an extremely rewarding enterprise, one that generates benefits for all involved. Students benefit because they learn more effective ways to fashion the positive futures they have come to college to create. Colleges and universities benefit because retention improves. Instructors benefit because they have the gratifying experience of assisting students to change their lives for the better . . . and that, I suggest, is our greatest mission as educators, regardless of our specific job description.

Intended Courses for *On Course*

With its emphasis on making wise choices and on writing guided journals, *On Course* is appropriate for use in a variety of courses. It is ideal for use in student success courses that seek to help students write more effectively. And *On Course* is perfect for writing courses that seek to help students achieve greater success in college and in life. Let's look more closely at how *On Course* supports the goals of both student success and writing courses.

Student Success Courses

On Course is designed for use in freshman seminars, student success courses, personal growth classes, self-awareness courses, college orientations, and all courses intended to assist students with their personal, academic, and professional success. By reading and writing about proven success strategies, students discover many new options for improving all aspects of their lives. Specifically, *On Course* invites students to explore how they can . . .

- Accept Greater Personal Responsibility
- Discover Self-Motivation
- Master Effective Self-Management Strategies
- Develop Mutually Supportive Relationships
- Change Self-Defeating Patterns and Limiting Beliefs
- Become Lifelong Learners
- Develop Emotional Intelligence
- Raise Their Self-Esteem
- Learn Effective Study Strategies
- Develop Critical and Creative Thinking

Writing Courses

On Course is also intended for use in developmental writing courses, freshman composition courses, and courses in personal or journal writing. As students write the guided journal entries in *On Course*, they get extensive practice in the same composition skills that accompanied writers use to create effective prose. The directions of the guided journals steer novice writers through the essential elements of the writing process:

1. **Prewriting (invention) strategies,** choices for focusing on a topic and generating ideas about it through various heuristic devices.
2. **Drafting strategies,** choices for organizing, developing, and expressing the ideas gathered during the invention stage.
3. **Revising strategies,** choices for rewriting the work done during the drafting stage.

By practicing this process in each journal entry, students are able to internalize the strategies and language skills necessary for college-level writing. In a community of fellow journal writers, students are motivated to write more effectively as they learn to live more effectively. Additionally, the journal entries in *On Course* give students compelling and motivating subject matter to explore in their formal writing assignments.

Unique Benefits of the Text

Regardless of the course in which it is used, *On Course* assists students to experience . . .

- **greater success in college and in life.** The success strategies that students learn and apply will improve the outcomes they create in all areas of their lives.
- **increased motivation and class participation.** Once students see improved results, they become more involved with their reading, writing, and class discussions. As students become personally involved, they learn firsthand the value of an active learning style.
- **better understanding of the writing process.** The guided journals introduce students to the writing process of successful writers; they learn the writing process by using it.
- **improved writing skills.** Journal writing offers students extensive practice in effective writing skills. Journal entries become the source of personally meaningful ideas that students can transform into formal essays of substance. (Later in this resource manual, suggestions for essay topics are provided for each chapter.)
- **the power of choice.** Students learn how to make wise choices that can dramatically improve the outcomes of their lives.
- **many voices from the realms of applied psychology and personal effectiveness** (through numerous marginal quotations).

Changes in the Fourth Edition

The essence of the first three editions has been maintained:

1. Short readings about proven **success strategies**.
2. **Guided journal entries** that encourage students to become active, responsible learners as they apply the success strategies to their lives.

3. **Case Studies for Critical Thinking** offer students an opportunity to apply their understanding of key success principles (like self-responsibility, self-motivation, and self-management) to real-life situations.
4. More than 150 effective **study skills** strategies for improving academic success in college, including sections on College Customs, Writing, Reading, Note Taking, Memorizing, Studying, and Test Taking.
5. "On Course at Work" essays in each chapter, showing students how each *On Course* principle will improve chances for success in their career.

Enhancing this foundation are the following new features in the fourth edition:

1. Strategies for effective money management.
2. Expanded information about stress management techniques.
3. **New cartoons and marginal quotations,** reinforcing the *On Course* success principles.
4. **Technology Exercises** have been added to the Wise-Choices feature to encourage the use of technology and the Internet.

Using *On Course*

On Course allows instructors maximum flexibility in its use. It can be used as either a primary or supplementary text. As a primary text, *On Course* stimulates lively class activities, including discussions of the success strategies, in-class readings of students' journal entries, exploration of the writing process, and experiential exercises (described later in this resource manual). When *On Course* is used as a supplementary text, the majority of in-class time can be devoted to instruction in study skills, life skills, writing skills (or whatever), while the students read the text and write their journal entries outside of class. Students will find the book easy to read and the directions for the guided journals easy to follow.

Naturally you will want to adapt *On Course* to your own style of teaching. In the sections that follow, I offer my thoughts on some of the issues you will certainly consider as you design your course.

Reading Student Journals

I collect journals early and often, weekly if possible. I give students immediate feedback to get them off to a good start. I don't read everything the students write; rather, I thumb through their journals to verify completion of each assigned journal entry and to give credit for a job thoroughly done. I do read journal entries that catch my eye. This reading gives me a sense of some of the issues that each student is facing. In a writing course, I also look for the writing problems with which each student needs help.

Whatever *you* decide in regard to reading journals, I have found it wise to let students know my intentions at the outset of the course.

Responding to Student Journals

Some instructors believe they must comment on everything their students write. Others believe just as strongly that journal writing is a private act and they have no business intruding upon this personal monologue.

I find myself falling somewhere in the middle of this debate. If I come across an idea that intrigues me, I write a response, encouragement, or question in the margin. The question I ask most often is "Can you dive deeper here?" Then I write a couple of questions that would assist the student to do just that. In some cases I write my comment on a *Post-it* note and press the note to the page; this approach gives the writer the choice to discard my comments or save them to show to his or her grandchildren. I also invite my students to ask for specific feedback by turning down the corner of a page and writing me a note.

Respecting Privacy

I see no way to keep totally private the personal thoughts that students express in a journal written for a college class. In fact, I alert them that both I and, occasionally, their classmates will be reading their journals. However, I do make (and recommend that you make) one important accommodation to privacy: I tell students that if they write an entry that they absolutely don't want others to read, they can fold the pages over and staple them at the bottom and the top. I give them my word that I will not read entries that have been stapled, although I do reserve the right to verify that there is, in fact, writing on the locked pages. I limit the number of locked journal entries to three and award locked journal entries the average score of all graded journals.

Helping Students with Personal Problems

Occasionally a student will reveal in his or her journal a serious personal problem that is beyond my expertise. I refer this student to an appropriate resource for assistance.

However, I suggest that you first talk to the student privately. Express your concern and your lack of training in the area of concern. Ask if the student would like you to connect him or her with someone who is trained to assist with the problem. I have yet to find a student refuse such a referral. I believe the keys to getting the student to agree to accept help are to (1) demonstrate a genuine caring for the student's welfare and a candid concern about the problem, (2) explain fully why you are recommending the person you want the student to see, and (3) offer to go with the student and introduce him or her to the person.

One last point. Some instructors with no training in counseling feel uncomfortable upon encountering a student's personal problems. I felt this way in the past myself. I believed that the student's personal life was none of my business. Today I have a different view. I don't teach subjects; I teach students. I teach them strategies for living rich, full lives. Sometimes those strategies are how to write a compelling essay and sometimes those strategies are how to be successful in college and in life. Anything that interferes with my student's success is of concern to me. Some students won't be around to learn my academic subjects if I don't initiate an intervention into their personal problems. The problem will be there whether I read about it or not; if I get to read about a problem in a student's journal, I have an opportunity to help a student transform a problem into a powerful learning experience.

Grading the Course

My intention is to give students as much control over their final grade as possible. I want them to choose the grade they want, then perform the actions necessary to earn that grade. I believe this approach shows students that they are responsible both for what they learn and for the grades they earn.

The sample syllabi that appear later in this Introduction offer specific examples of how you might put students in control of earning their grades. Meanwhile, here are some general suggestions for determining student grades:

Journal Entries I don't believe that the spirit of writing a journal is compatible with grading students' ideas or writing styles, but I do believe in rewarding students for their efforts. In my grading system (explained in greater detail later), I award up to 5 points for each journal entry. For entries that are lacking in completeness and/or quality of response I give a score between 1 and 4. I award 5 points for each entry that is complete and that demonstrates a commendable effort to explore in depth the issues at hand. For an extraordinary effort that goes above and beyond the expected, I have been known to lose my head and award a 6 or 7. After I check journals the first time, I invite students to revise any entries for a higher score; this one-time offer allows them to discover and adjust to my evaluation standards without a penalty to their final grade.

Quizzes Occasional quizzes on readings have at least three benefits: (1) They can motivate students to stay up-to-date in their assignments, (2) They give students immediate feedback about whether they understand a concept that is being explored, (3) They are great practice for what students will face in other classes. *Quiz questions appear in this manual at the end of each chapter discussion.*

Essays In both a student success course and a writing course, I ask students to transform their personal journal writings into formal public writings. *Formal writing assignment topics appear in this manual at the end of each chapter discussion.*

You might also want to be on the alert for formal writing assignments that are appropriate for an individual student. For example, during a discussion about learning styles (Journal Entry #23), one of my students discussed how some of her high school teachers had "made" her dislike school. She expressed such outrage at her experience that I encouraged her to write a formal letter to the superintendent of her school district and express her experience, her anger, and her suggestions. (I accepted this assignment as a substitute for another class assignment.) She took me up on my offer and produced her best piece of formal writing for the entire semester.

Tests In my courses, I consider both journals and essays to be take-home tests. I believe that the most valuable examinations are those that not only evaluate a student's knowledge but give the student an opportunity to apply his or her knowledge in a real-life situation. Whether you prefer giving tests in class or as homework, I recommend using essay questions like the ones at the end of each chapter in this manual.

Sample Syllabi

What follows is a sample syllabus for a 45-hour student success course conducted over a 15-week semester. Some instructors use it exactly as is; others adapt it to their particular needs.

Syllabus for a Student Success Course

Welcome! My goal in this course is to offer you one of the most valuable learning experiences of your entire life. And I need your full cooperation to make it work!

Course Purpose: This course is designed to help you create greater success in college and in life. In the coming weeks, you will learn many proven strategies for creating greater academic, professional, and personal success. We will use guided journal writings to explore these strategies, and as a bonus, you will learn to express yourself more effectively in writing. You may never again have an opportunity quite like this one to discover how to create a rich, personally fulfilling life. I urge you to make the most of this extraordinary opportunity! If you do, you will dramatically change the outcome of your life—for the better!

Course Objectives: In this course, you will learn how to . . .

1. **Take charge of your life.** You will learn how to take greater personal responsibility, gaining more control over the outcomes that you create both in college and in life.
2. **Increase self-motivation.** You will learn to create greater inner motivation by discovering your own personally meaningful goals and dreams.
3. **Improve personal self-management.** You will learn numerous strategies for taking control of your time and energy, allowing you to move more effectively and efficiently toward the accomplishment of your goals and dreams.
4. **Develop interdependence.** You will learn how to develop mutually supportive relationships with people who will help you achieve your goals and dreams as you assist them to achieve theirs.
5. **Increase self-awareness.** You will learn how to understand and revise your self-defeating patterns of behavior, thought, and emotion as well as your unconscious limiting beliefs.
6. **Maximize your learning.** You will discover the natural process of effective learning and understand how to apply that process according to your individual learning style preference. This knowledge will enable you not only to get better grades in college but also to be a more effective lifelong learner.
7. **Develop emotional intelligence.** You will learn effective strategies for managing your emotional life, decreasing stress and distress while increasing your inner sense of well-being.
8. **Raise your self-esteem.** You will learn how to develop self-acceptance, self-confidence, self-respect, self-love, and unconditional self-worth.
9. **Write more effectively.** You will learn how to improve your writing skills through the extensive writing practice offered by your guided journal entries.
10. **Improve creative and critical thinking skills.** You will learn how to enhance the thinking skills essential for analyzing and solving problems in your academic, professional, and personal lives.
11. **Master effective study skills.** You will learn how to raise your grades in college by improving essential skills like reading, note taking, memorizing, studying, and test taking.
12. **Manage your money.** You will learn helpful techniques for increasing your income (including gaining more financial aid for college) and decreasing your expenses.

Course Supplies:
1. *On Course*, Fourth Edition, by Skip Downing
2. String-bound composition notebook (or computer journal on disk with entries printed and placed in a 3-ring binder)

Method: By reading *On Course* (our textbook), you'll learn empowering strategies that have helped others create great success. By keeping a guided journal, you'll discover how to apply these success strategies to achieve your own goals and dreams. By participating in class activities and focused conversations, and by completing a course project, you will further improve your ability to stay on course to your success. Once you make these new strategies your own through application, you'll have the ability to dramatically improve the outcome of your life—academically, professionally, and personally.

Course Grades:

		Points
A	=	270–300
B	=	240–269
C	=	210–239
D	=	180–209
F	=	179 or below

Course Projects:

	Points
1. 15 Quizzes (5 points each)	75
2. 31 Success Journal entries (5 points each)	155
3. 1 Personal Philosophy of Success Essay	70
Total Possible Points	300

Each of these three components of your grade is explained below.

1. Quizzes (75 Possible Points)

This is a course for students who wish to be successful in college and in life. One of the most important factors of success in any endeavor is consistent and active participation. To encourage and reward your preparation for active participation at every class, fifteen unannounced quizzes on the readings will be given. If you have read the assignment and completed your journal entry, you should have no trouble earning the maximum points (5) for each quiz. **No quiz may be made up.**

Great success is created one small step at a time. Each time that you earn your quiz points you take an important step toward your success in this course . . . and in life!

2. Success Journals (155 Possible Points)

Your Success Journal provides an opportunity to explore your thoughts and feelings as you experiment with the success strategies presented in *On Course.* By carefully examining each strategy in your journal, you will discover which ones will assist you to create a rich, personally fulfilling life. Although I will be collecting your journals and looking through them, **write your journal for yourself,** not for me. Your journal entries will occasionally be read by your classmates.

Journal Writings: During this semester, you will write in your composition notebook thirty-one numbered journal entries from our textbook. These entries will be written outside of class. Additionally, you will write occasional lettered journal entries based on class exercises. These entries will be written in class. At various times you will have an opportunity to read a journal entry to one or more classmates. **THEREFORE, PLEASE BRING YOUR TEXTBOOK AND JOURNAL TO EVERY CLASS.**

Note: If you wish, you may write the first draft of journal entries on loose sheets of paper, but *all journal entries must be written in the composition notebook when it is handed in for evaluation.* Or if you choose to write your journal on a computer, you will print hard copies of all entries and bring them to class neatly organized in a 3-ring binder. This requirement will assure that none of your entries gets lost. At the end of this semester, you will have your entire journal to keep for years to come. Many students come to regard their personal journal as one of their most valued possessions.

Journal Evaluations: I will collect your journals weekly. You may pick up your journal in the departmental office forty-eight hours later. It is not my intention to read every journal entry you write. Instead, I will look through your journal book to verify the completion of each assignment and to give credit for a job well done. I read occasional journal entries to get a sense of the issues you are working on. With this knowledge I can be of greater assistance to you this semester.

If you want my comment on a specific part of your journal, simply turn down the corner of the appropriate page. On that page, write a note about the response you desire from me.

Privacy: Occasionally you may write a journal entry that you wish to keep private. If so, simply fold the appropriate pages over and staple them closed at the top and bottom. You have my word that I will respect your privacy. I do reserve the right to confirm that there is, in fact, writing on these pages. You may lock up to three journal entries; more than that will require my permission. Locked journal entries will be given scores equal to the average score of all other journal entries.

Journal Points: Each journal entry will be awarded up to 5 points. Thus, all thirty-one journal entries will be worth a possible total of 155 points. A journal entry will be awarded the maximum of 5 points if it fulfills the following two criteria:

1. The entry is *complete* (all steps in the directions have been responded to), and
2. The entry is *written with high standards* (an obvious attempt has been made to *dive deep*).

Grammar, spelling, and punctuation will NOT be factors in awarding points in this journal. You are free to express yourself without concern for standard English conventions.

IMPORTANT NOTE: All thirty-one journal entries must be completed to earn a passing grade in the course.

3. Personal Philosophy of Success Essay (70 Possible Points)

As your final project, you will write an essay in which you present your own Personal Philosophy of Success. The purpose of your essay is to define the success strategies that you will use for years to come. This essay is your opportunity to write the script that will keep you on course to a rich, personally fulfilling life! *The minimum length of this essay is 1500 words, and it must be prepared on a word processor.*

An "A" paper will . . .

1. Demonstrate the writer's careful consideration of three or more important success strategies.
2. Contain extensive support (examples, experiences, evidence, and/or explanation) for each strategy, and
3. Show a commitment to excellence in preparation, including professional appearance and a command of standard English.

   Your Philosophy of Success Essay must be completed to earn a passing grade in the course.

Course Rules for Success

To create the very best environment for supporting your success and the success of your classmates, this course has three important rules. The more challenging these rules are for you, the more value you will experience by adopting them. By choosing to follow these three rules, you are choosing to be successful not only in this course but in your life. These rules will support your success in every goal you pursue!

1. **Show up!** To support my success, I choose to attend every scheduled class period in its entirety.
2. **Do the work!** To support my success, I choose to do my very best work in preparing all of my assignments and hand them in on time.
3. **Participate actively!** To support my success, I choose to stay mentally alert in every class, offering my best comments, questions, and answers when appropriate.

Student Success Course Schedule of Assignments (15-Week Course)

REMINDER: Fifteen unannounced quizzes will be given. No quizzes may be made up.

Assignments below are due at the first class of the week in which they are due. *Bring your textbook and journal to every class.*

Week 1:	*On Course:* Read/Write Journal #1
	Read: Learning College Customs
Week 2:	*On Course:* Read/Write Journals #2 and 3
Week 3:	*On Course:* Read/Write Journals #4 and 5
	Read: Effective Writing
Week 4:	*On Course:* Read/Write Journals #6, 7, and 8
Week 5:	*On Course:* Read/Write Journals #9 and 10
	Read: Effective Reading
Week 6:	*On Course:* Read/Write Journals #11, 12, and 13
Week 7:	*On Course:* Read/Write Journals # 14 and 15
	Read: Effective Money Management
Week 8:	*On Course:* Read/Write Journals #16, 17, and 18
Week 9:	*On Course:* Read/Write Journals #19 and 20
	Read: Effective Note Taking
Week 10:	*On Course:* Read/Write Journals #21, 22, and 23
Week 11:	*On Course:* Read/Write Journals # 24 and 25
	Read: Effective Memorizing
Week 12:	*On Course:* Read/Write Journals #26, 27, and 28
Week 13:	*On Course:* Read/Write Journals #29 and 30
	Read: Effective Studying
Week 14:	*On Course:* Read/Write Journal #31
	Read: Effective Test Taking
Week 15:	"Philosophy of Success" Essay Due

Syllabus for a Writing Course

Welcome! My goal in this course is to offer you one of the most valuable learning experiences of your entire life. And I need your full cooperation to make it work!

Course Purpose: The purpose of this course is to offer you the opportunity to learn powerful writing strategies. The theme of our class is **SUCCESS** . . . what it is and how can we achieve it. In the coming weeks, you will learn many proven strategies for living a rich, personally fulfilling life. We will use writing to explore these strategies, and through this practice, you will learn to express yourself more effectively in writing.

Course Objectives: Specifically, by the end of this course, successful students (YOU!) will be able to write essays that

1. are controlled by a clear **purpose**,
2. develop that purpose with sufficient, well-organized **support**,
3. adapt the purpose and support to a particular **audience**, and
4. are written in a smooth, grammatically appropriate **style**.

Method: In this course, you will be reading, writing, and talking about how to create success (as you define it). You will keep a guided journal in which you will explore many strategies of success. Five times during the course you will write a formal essay based on the ideas you have been developing in your journal.

Once you make both these writing and success strategies your own, you will have the ability to dramatically improve the outcome of your life.

Course Supplies:
1. *On Course* by Skip Downing
2. String-bound composition notebook (or computer journal on disk with entries printed and placed in a 3-ring binder)

Course Grades:

		Points
A	=	477–530
B	=	424–476
C	=	371–423
D	=	318–370
F	=	317 or below

Course Projects:

	Points
1. 15 Quizzes (5 points each)	75
2. 31 Success Journal entries (5 points each)	155
3. 5 Essays (60 points each)	300
Total Possible Points	530

Each of these three projects is explained below.

1. Quizzes (75 Possible Points)

[For explanatory text, see the equivalent section in the sample Student Success Course Syllabus in this resource manual (p. xv).]

2. Success Journals (155 Possible Points)

[For explanatory text, see the equivalent section in the sample Student Success Course Syllabus in this resource manual (p. xv).]

3. Formal Essays (300 Possible Points)

Purpose: Five times during the semester you will turn in a formal essay. In these essays, you will take ideas explored in your private journal and write them for a public audience. In this manner, you will practice and demonstrate the essay-writing skills that we will be learning in this course. Topics will be provided, but you are invited to offer alternative topics that appeal to you. Alternative topics must be approved before you write the essay. The minimum length of each essay is 750 words, and it must be prepared on a word processor.

Each essay will be awarded up to 60 points. An essay earning 60 points will:

1. Be controlled by a clear purpose,
2. Develop that purpose with sufficient, well-organized support,
3. Adapt the purpose and support to a particular audience, and
4. Show a commitment to excellence in preparation, including professional appearance and use of standard English.

Essays will be penalized 5 points for each day late. You must complete all five essays to earn a passing grade in the course.

Course Rules for Success

[For explanatory text, see the equivalent section in the sample Student Success Course Syllabus in this resource manual (p. xvii).]

Writing Course Schedule of Assignments (15-Week Course)

NOTE: Fifteen unannounced quizzes will be given. No quizzes may be made up. Assignments below are listed here on the day they are due in class. *Bring your textbook and journal to every class.*

Week 1:	*On Course:* Read/Write Journal #1	
Week 2:	*On Course:* Read/Write Journals #2 and 3	**Essay #1 Due**
Week 3:	*On Course:* Read/Write Journals #4, 5, and 6	
Week 4:	*On Course:* Read/Write Journals #7, 8, and 9	
Week 5:	*On Course:* Read/Write Journals #10 and 11	**Essay #2 Due**
Week 6:	*On Course:* Read/Write Journals #12, 13, and 14	
Week 7:	*On Course:* Read/Write Journals # 15 and 16	

Week 8:	*On Course:* Read/Write Journals #17 and 18	**Essay #3 Due**
Week 9:	*On Course:* Read/Write Journals #19 and 20	
Week 10:	*On Course:* Read/Write Journals #21, 22, and 23	
Week 11:	*On Course:* Read/Write Journals # 24 and 25	**Essay #4 Due**
Week 12:	*On Course:* Read/Write Journals #26, 27, and 28	
Week 13:	*On Course:* Read/Write Journals #29 and 30	
Week 14:	*On Course:* Read/Write Journal #31	
Week 15:		**Essay #5 Due**

Adapting *On Course* to Shorter Semesters or Quarters

Chapters 1, 2, and 3 present concepts and vocabulary that are foundational for all subsequent chapters. Chapter 6 presents concepts and vocabulary that are fundamental for work in Chapters 7 and 8. Chapter 9 offers students a second opportunity to take the self-assessment questionnaire that they took in Chapter 1. By comparing the results of these two questionnaires, students can see evidence of the changes in their behaviors, thoughts, emotions, and beliefs.

Consequently, I would suggest that you follow one of three plans if you assign students fewer than all thirty-one journal entries.

Plan 1: Start with Chapter 1 and go as far into the book as time allows. Then assign Journal #31 at the end for the post-course questionnaire. For example, if you have a 15-week course that meets 1 hour per week (15 hours), you might assign the following 15 journals:

Journals #1–14 and #31

Additionally, you could assign some or all of the study skill sections entitled "Wise Choices in College" and "Case Study for Critical Thinking," and the "On Course at Work" essays.

Plan 2: Assign foundational Chapters 1, 2, 3, and 6 and as many other chapters as time allows. For example, if you have a 15-week course that meets 2 hours per week (30 hours), you might assign the following 22 journals:

Chapters 1–4 (Journals #1–14)
Chapter 6 (Journals #19–21)
Chapter 7 (Journals #23–26)
Chapter 9 (Journal #31)

Additionally, you could assign some or all of the study skill sections entitled "Wise Choices in College" and "Case Study for Critical Thinking," and the "On Course at Work" essays.

Plan 3: Assign foundational Chapters 1, 2, 3, and 6 and as many other individual journals as time allows. For example, if you have a 12-week course that meets 2.5 hours per week (30 hours), you might assign the following 25 journals:

Chapters 1–3 (Journals #1–10)
Journals #12, 14, 15, 16
Chapter 6 (Journals #19–21)
Journals #23, 24, 25, 27, 28, 29, 30, 31

Additionally, you could assign some or all of the study skill sections entitled "Wise Choices in College" and "Case Study for Critical Thinking," and the "On Course at Work" essays.

Creating a Learner-Centered Classroom

The remainder of this manual offers numerous suggestions for classroom activities. Each suggestion is intended to promote your students' active inquiry. Within every class, students will ideally experience two or more of the following activities:

1. An exercise or case study
2. A brief, timed freewriting activity in their journals (these freewritings can be lettered to contrast with the numbered journals from *On Course*)
3. A discussion (in pairs, trios, quartets, or entire class)
4. Lecture/instruction (from the instructor, a student, guest speaker, or video)
5. Exploration of study skills strategies
6. A quiz

Let's take a look at each of these six activities:

1. **Exercises and Case Studies:** In most class periods, you will want to provide students with some sort of a motivating experience to get their energy flowing in the direction of the day's topic. Later in this manual, you will find directions for many dynamic exercises and case study activities. Here, I would like to offer some all-purpose exercises that can be used to generate discussion within any chapter.

   A. *Journal Readings:* Students sit in pairs. (1) Student A reads a designated journal entry to Student B. (2) Student B responds to Student A, "What I hear you saying in this entry is . . ." (3) Students now reverse roles and repeat Steps 1 and 2. (4) Students then take a few minutes to discuss or freewrite any thoughts or feelings that came up for them as they read or listened. (5) The class discusses what they experienced and learned during the entire process.

   This activity, simple as it is, may be the most powerful exercise I have to offer. It seldom fails to energize students' thinking, and it generates many benefits: (1) Readers hear their own ideas, often discovering how to take their thinking to deeper, more complex levels. (2) Readers hear their own voice, noting where their writing is clear, where muddy. As a result they improve as editors of their own writing. (3) Responders get to hear another person's slant on the same issue they have explored, an experience that often helps them develop critical and creative thinking (and also makes them more aware of the importance of audience in communication). (4) Responders learn to practice active listening, which allows them to more effectively discover the heart of any communication. This is especially valuable for reinforcing the listening skills that students will learn in Journal Entry #17. (5) The sharing of ideas by readers and responders creates community among class members, which often raises their level of commitment to the activities and learnings available in the course. I **HIGHLY RECOMMEND THIS EXERCISE!**

   B. *Quotations:* Students choose a quotation from the margins of *On Course* with which they agree or disagree. They do a short (2–4 minute) freewriting response to their chosen quote. Students then share their responses in pairs (as in Exercise A), small groups, or with the entire class. This exercise heightens students' awareness of what others (famous and not-so-famous) have said about the success strategies being considered.

   C. *Poems:* Students read and respond in a short freewriting to one of the poems. Students then share their responses in pairs (as in Exercise A), in small groups, or with the entire class. This exercise encourages students to overcome their resistance to poetry. They see that poets use special modes of language that students can use in their own writings.

D. *Cartoons:* Students read a cartoon and respond in a short writing to the question, "What does this cartoon say about being successful?" Students then share their responses in pairs (as in Exercise A), small groups, or with the entire class. This exercise enables students to see the humor in serious topics, as well as the seriousness of humorous topics. And it's fun! (A variation is to have students find and bring in their own cartoons that illuminate one of the strategies of success being considered.)

E. *Focus Questions:* Students read the focus questions that precede each of the thirty-one text sections and write their best present answers to the questions. Students then share their responses in pairs (as in Exercise A), in small groups, or with the entire class. This exercise enables students to preview the success strategies they are about to consider and discover what they already think and know about the topic. The point should also be made that reading the article through the filter of questions enables a reader to gain more valuable (usable) information. This exercise assists students to become better readers. It is wise to emphasize the focus questions early in the semester so students get in the habit of thinking about them before beginning to read.

F. *Chapter-Opening Charts (Successful Students/Struggling Students):* Students read the summary chart preceding an upcoming chapter and respond in a short writing to the questions, "Which of these choices do you think will be easiest for you? The most difficult?" Students then share their responses in pairs (as in Exercise A), in small groups, or with the entire class. As in the consideration of focus questions, this exercise enables students to preview the success strategies they are about to consider. Once again, the point should be made that reading through the filter of questions and personal application enables the reader to gain more valuable (usable) information.

2. **Freewriting:** Class discussions are usually improved when students first freewrite briefly about the issue under consideration. This activity gives reflective learners time to gather and organize their thoughts for discussion. Such in-class writings can be lettered in students' journals to distinguish them from the numbered journal entries from *On Course.* I recommend timing these writings, starting with short sessions (1 or 2 minutes) early in the semester and lengthening them to perhaps 10 minutes toward the end of the semester. Typical directions to the students are as follows: *When I say, "Go," begin writing about _____ until I say, "Stop." There is no right or wrong thing to write. Simply follow your thoughts and feelings about this issue wherever they lead. If your mind goes blank at any time, write, "My mind is blank. . . . I can't think of anything to write. . . . What am I going to do? My mind is still blank. . . . Let's see—what am I supposed to write about here? Oh, yes, . . ."* Eventually, your mind will probably return to the task at hand. If not, whatever you write is fine. Any questions? Ready, begin.* Students soon learn that freewriting is a powerful prewriting (or prediscussion) strategy for generating ideas.

3. **Discussions:** Discussions (in pairs, trios, quartets, or the entire class) are usually quite lively when preceded by a stimulating exercise and/or freewriting. Before entertaining a discussion by the entire class, you may wish to put the students in smaller groups (two, three, or four) for a warm-up discussion. Introverted or shy students are more likely to participate in these small groups and, after this dress rehearsal, may be more inclined to express their ideas to the whole class. Each exercise in this manual offers suggested questions for stimulating meaningful class discussions. However, one all-purpose discussion technique is the PMI format suggested by Edward de Bono in his book *De Bono's Thinking Course. P* stands for Plus (the good points of an idea), *M* stands for Minus (the bad points of an idea), and *I* stands for Interesting (the intriguing points of an idea). To do a PMI discussion, simply explore these three elements of any idea, one at a time.

4. **Lecture/Instruction:** Once students' mental juices are flowing (after the exercises, freewritings, and/or discussions), they are ripe for further instruction. For some topics, you can assign students the role of instructor and let them instruct the class themselves. This approach gives students ultimate responsibility for their own education. Guest speakers or videos also add a nice change of pace.

5. **Exploration of Study Skills Strategies:** At the end of each "Wise Choices in College" section is an exercise that will help students practice the specific study skill they have been learning. Here, however, is a collaborative learning activity that can be used with any of the study skills sections.

A. Put students in "home" groups of three, each with a copy of *On Course* open to the study skill section you are working on. You may have assigned the reading for homework, or you may have students seeing it for the first time.

B. Point out to students that the menu of study skills strategies is divided into three sections: Before, During, and After. Ask each student in a trio to choose one section.

C. Say to students, "Take the next ten minutes to decide which you think are the **three** most valuable strategies in your section and how you would teach these strategies to others."

D. Have the students now move into three "expert" groups by the section they have chosen: Before, During, and After. Say to students, "In your expert group, you have twenty minutes to decide which are the three most important strategies in your section and prepare yourselves to return to your home groups and teach these three strategies to your two partners."

E. Have the students return to their home groups. Say, "Now, going in order of Before, During, and After, teach your partners one strategy. After each of you has taught one strategy, continue going around, teaching additional strategies until I call time."

F. As a final step, you can ask students, "What new strategies will you commit to experimenting with?" Because each of us has preferences for the way we learn best, encourage students to experiment with various strategies, making those that improve their results in college part of their repertoire of study skills.

6. **Quizzes:** Frequent quizzes motivate students to come to class prepared, and they act as a great review of the reading. I recommend having students exchange and grade quizzes in class so they get immediate feedback. Quiz questions for every journal topic appear later in this manual.

Using the Exercises in This Manual

We are now about to turn our attention to the nine chapters of *On Course* and explore the class exercises that will make for an involving learning environment.

First, however, let's take a moment to look at how you might use the class exercises. To do so, let's preview the six parts of the exercise directions.

Purpose: Each exercise begins with a statement of the outcome(s) that the activity is intended to produce. This feature allows you to make a quick determination as to whether a particular activity is appropriate for your course.

Supplies and Setup: These directions tell you what supplies (if any) are needed for the exercise; most of the supplies are common items that you probably already own or to which you have easy access. Setup instructions indicate anything that has to be arranged before the exercise begins.

Directions: [Directions to the instructor are written in brackets—like this.] *Words of direction that you might speak to the students are italicized—like this.* Directions labeled "Optional" may be dropped to save time.

One essential point about directions: The success of an exercise is dependent on whether students fully understand the directions. I recommend confirming that every student is clear on the directions before commencing with the actual activity. One way to clarify directions even further is to give a demonstration (DEMO) of exactly what you are asking the students to do. *So, here's what that would look like . . . Is everyone clear on what to do? Okay, begin.*

Approximate Time: Each step in the directions has an approximate time indicated. These times are guidelines and can be adapted to your circumstances or time restraints. If the exercise is running long, you can shorten the discussion. If the exercise is running short, you can lengthen the discussion.

Instructor Notes: Sometimes there are special aspects of an exercise that are not part of the directions but that I have found make the activity more successful. I write these to myself after doing the activity so I'll remember them for next time. I have included my "Instructor Notes" here, and I suggest you add your own after you use an exercise.

Source: Where appropriate, I have indicated my source for an exercise. In most cases, even if I have learned the idea from someone else, I have adapted it to my own style. I urge you to do the same. Make each exercise your own.

On Course Newsletter

Subscribe to the *On Course* Newsletter and receive FREE weekly emails (biweekly in the summer) with innovative strategies for empowering your students to become active, responsible, and successful learners. Edited by Skip Downing, this newsletter makes a great supplement to this Facilitator's Manual and is like a professional development workshop on your desktop. To subscribe, simply send an email to *oncourse-on@mail-list.com.* You don't even have to type anything. The newsletter computer will automatically subscribe your return address.

For additional classroom activities and out-of-class assignments, you can visit the *On Course* Web Site at *www.OnCourseWorkshop.com.* Here you will find a large collection of student success strategies that work extremely well in the *On Course* classroom.

Ancillaries for *On Course*

New! Houghton Mifflin Class Prep CD-ROM provides instructors with electronic support to accompany the *Facilitator's Manual* for *On Course.* Available for both Windows and Macintosh platforms, the CD-ROM provides sample syllabi, journal topics, additional exercises, quizzes, and more helpful tips and strategies for using *On Course* in your course. Also included on the CD-ROM are **PowerPoint** presentations created by the author to accompany your teaching of *On Course.*

College Survival Web Site (*http://collegesurvival.college.hmco.com/*): This comprehensive web site offers additional materials to further practice the strategies taught in *On Course.* The web site includes an interactive version of the Self-Assessment as well as additional exercises, articles, and links to outside resources.

Houghton Mifflin College Survival Supplements and Resources

College Survival Consulting Services: For more than fifteen years, Houghton Mifflin's College Survival consultants have provided consultation and training for the design, implementation, and presentation of student-success and first-year courses. Our team of consultants has a wide variety of experience in teaching and administering the first-year course. They can provide help in establishing or improving your student-success program. We offer assistance in course design, instructor training, teaching strategies, annual conferences, and much more. Contact College Survival today at 1-800-528-8323, or visit us on the Web at *http://collegesurvival.college.hmco.com/instructors.*

College Survival Conferences: College Survival provides faculty development and educational opportunities for teachers, student services personnel, orientation coordinators, curriculum designers, and administrators. We invite all those involved with enhancing instruction and improving students' persistence and performance to attend our workshops/conferences. Sessions are presented by experienced student-success educators and first-year program coordinators from across the United States and Canada, as well as by College Survival consultants, trainers, and authors. Client schools using a Houghton Mifflin College Survival title as a required text can register two people free and additional persons at a discounted fee. Colleges are encouraged to send teams from strategic areas to get the maximum benefit.

Houghton Mifflin Success Planner is a week-at-a-glance academic planner available in a specially priced package with this text. Produced in partnership with Premier, the Success Planner assists students in managing their time both on and off campus. The planner includes a "Survival Kit" of helpful success tips from Houghton Mifflin Company College Survival textbooks.

The **HM Assessment and Portfolio Builder CD-ROM** is a personal assessment tool to assist students in preparing for the workplace. Students will build their portfolio by responding to questions in the modules Personal, Interpersonal, Career, and Community, and by reflecting on their skills, attitudes, values, and behaviors. The Accomplishments Report will summarize the results of their responses, perfect for creating a résumé or preparing for interviews. Equipped with their accomplishments report, students are invited to explore Houghton Mifflin's web-based **Career Resource Center** for more tips, exercises, articles, and ideas to help them succeed on their journey from college to career. The Bridge from College to Career lets students practice new skills in college that can be applied as they enter the job market. Finding the Perfect Job helps students fine-tune their résumé-writing and interviewing skills. And Skills for Your Future provides strategies in problem solving and decision making to help students learn how to work with others and communicate on the job. (ISBN: 0-618-23283-4)

Myers-Briggs Type Indicator (MBTI) Instrument: This is the most widely used personality inventory in history—shrink-wrapped with *On Course* for a discounted price at qualified schools. The standard Form M self-scorable instrument contains 93 items that determine preferences on four scales: Extroversion—Introversion, Sensing—Intuition, Thinking—Feeling, and Judging—Perceiving.

Retention Management System College Student Inventory: The Noel Levitz College Student Inventory instrument is available in a specially priced package with this text. This early-alert, early-intervention program identifies students with tendencies that contribute to dropping out of school. Students can participate in an integrated, campus-wide program. Advisors are sent three interpretive reports: The Student's Report, the Advisor/Counselor Report, and The College Summary and Planning Report.

Videos are available to supplement your in-class lectures. Contact your sales representative or College Survival Consultant for an up-to-date list of available videos and for pricing information. Here are just some of the videos we have to offer:

The Interviewing Process: Strategies for Making the Right Impression: This 30-minute video takes you through the interviewing process, from start to finish. From preparation—everything from what to wear, questions and answers to think about, research on the company—to the actual interview—in which you will see real-to-life interviewing scenarios—to what to do after the interview—evaluating how it went, seeing what you can learn, and following up, this video will give you the strategies to be successful in your next interview. (ISBN 0-618-37982-7)

Money and Finances Video: "Money and Finances" discusses strategies for students to use to help them gain control of their finances and overcome the money problems they may currently have. Students will hear advice from financial advisor Ann Egan on income and expenses, and will examine the general principles of budgeting and cash flow. Through real-world money challenges, presented by students like themselves, this video will teach your students to develop the skills of good money management, including the pitfalls of credit card spending and a discussion of financial aid. *Running Time:* approx. 30 min. (ISBN 0-618-38255-0)

Embrace Diversity: Begin a discussion of diversity in your classroom with this video to assist you in helping your students become more aware of how to embrace differences and similarities during interaction with their peers and co-workers. A diverse group of students representing multiple cultures, ages, races, and religious and ethnic backgrounds provide personal experience and show by example effective means of communicating across cultures. Students can learn to explore their personal biases through education and move toward removing preconceived notions and changing their attitudes to succeed at being open-minded and accepting of different perspectives. (ISBN 0-618-23279-6)

Roundtable Discussions videotapes: "Study Strategies" and "Life Skills." They are also ideal for independent use to promote student discussion and provide quick reinforcement of strategies and skills. In these videos, five students from diverse backgrounds and situations discuss and actively seek solutions to the problems they face in college and in life.

    Life Skills, (ISBN 0-395-74035-5)—This video is twenty-five minutes long, and covers goal setting, time management, and stress management.

    Study Strategies, (ISBN 0-395-74034-7)—Thirty-five minutes long, this video covers note taking, reading, memory, and test taking.

Special note to instructors: If you have questions about or suggestions for improving either *On Course* or this manual, please email me at *skipdown@starpower.net* or write me at the address below. I will be happy to acknowledge you as the source of any exercises or suggestions that are included in subsequent editions. For your students, I thank you for helping them live rich, personally fulfilling lives. May you experience the same.

Skip Downing
c/o Houghton Mifflin Student Success Programs
215 Park Avenue South, 11th Floor
New York, New York 10003

On Course Workshop

Empower Your Students
to Achieve their Greatest Success!

Learn practical strategies that engage your students in becoming active, responsible and successful learners at this highly interactive faculty development retreat. Designed for educators across disciplines who want to help students achieve their greatest potential—academically, personally, and professionally—this workshop will energize and inspire both your professional and personal life.

You'll learn:
- How to use the seven domains available to educators to motivate and transform students.
- Best practices from innovators in education, psychology, business, sports and personal effectiveness.
- New motivational strategies that appeal to a variety of learning styles.
- How these strategies improve academic success and student retention.

Whether you use *On Course* as your course text, or you simply want to revitalize your instruction techniques, this workshop is for you!

Graduate credits and CEUs are available!

- Visit *www.oncourseworkshop.com*—for workshop dates, locations, and registration information, and to view a sampling of classroom strategies, or
- Contact Skip Downing by email at *skipdown@starpower.net* or by phone at (888)597-6451 (toll-free) to register.

Chapter 1
Getting On Course to Your Success

Concept

If we are to get on course to our success, we must first determine where we are currently. By offering students an opportunity to assess their present strengths and weaknesses, we empower them with information that is essential to their success. Additionally, when we help students begin their academic journeys in an engaging way, we help them to give their best efforts. Students are more likely to commit to working hard in a course when they understand . . .

1. What the course is about,
2. Why the course is of personal value to them, and
3. How they can apply the information of the course to better their lives.

It is as necessary for students to feel comfortable in this course as it is important for them to learn what this course is about and how it will benefit them. When students feel at ease in the classroom, they are more likely to stretch out of their comfort zones and try new behaviors, beliefs, and attitudes. As we begin our journey in this course, our first goal is to create a learning environment that encourages students to change.

Empowers Students to . . .

1. Begin thinking about what it means to be successful.
2. Understand the value that they can create for themselves in the course.
3. Assess their strengths and weaknesses.
4. Comprehend the importance and the process of relaxation.
5. Risk change.

Remember to consider using the all-purpose exercises mentioned in the introduction, especially JOURNAL READINGS, QUOTATIONS, POEMS, CARTOONS, FOCUS QUESTIONS, AND CHAPTER-OPENING SUMMARIES. Remind students to use letters to label any in-class writing they do in their journals.

Journal 1.   Taking the First Step

EXERCISE 1-1: What's in a Name?

Purpose: To enable students to get to know their classmates and begin to create a comfortable learning community where students feel safe to risk new behaviors and adopt new beliefs and attitudes. This exercise also subtly lays the groundwork for later discussions of patterns.

Supplies and Setup: Pens and journals. (If students don't yet have journals, they can write on notebook paper and later copy this writing into their journal.)

Directions:

1. *Write your full name on the top of a blank page in your journal. Now, write the story of your name. Where did it come from? How do you feel about it? How do you think your name has influenced who you are? Add anything else that comes to mind about your name as you write.* [Teacher DEMOs by telling the story of his or her name.] [5–8 minutes]

2. [Move students into groups of 4.] *The person in your group who will have the next birthday goes first. That person reads the story of his or her name to the group. Then go clockwise around your group until each person has read. When everyone has finished reading, have a discussion about any patterns that you notice about the names in your group. For example, perhaps you'll find that many of you in your group were named for a relative or that most of you prefer a different name. Later, one of you will report on what your group discovered about your names. You have 10 minutes. Any questions? If not, please begin.* [10 minutes]

3. *Let's hear from each group's spokesperson. What did you learn about the names of the people in your group? Any patterns? Any unusual stories?* [5–15 minutes]

Approximate Time: 20–30 minutes

Instructor Notes:

1. This activity is a great first-day icebreaker, generating lively discussions. People love talking about their names. Some people discover thoughts and feelings about them that they didn't realize they had.

Source: Barbara Jaffe, El Camino Community College

EXERCISE 1-2: The Choices of Successful Students

Purpose: To identify the choices of successful students and have students see that they are capable of making these choices.

Supplies and Setup: Chalkboard (or blank overhead transparency or newsprint); students in groups of 4 or 5

Directions:

1. *In your group, create a list of the choices of successful students. In other words, what choices do successful students make that struggling students don't? Think about the choices you can see (outer behaviors) and the choices you can't see (inner attitudes/beliefs).* [5 minutes]

2. *Okay, let's hear what you came up with for the choices of successful students.* [Record the choices on the chalkboard.] [5 minutes]

3. *Which of these choices do you think are the most essential contributors to a student's success? Vote for three. As I call off a choice, raise your hand to cast your vote.* [Tally the votes each time, and record them next to the item on the list.] [5 minutes]

4. *Which of these choices are you willing to commit to so that you can be a successful student this semester? Make a list of them in your journal.* [5 minutes]

5. *Let's hear what you wrote.* [Invite students to stand and state the choices they commit to.] [5 minutes]

Approximate Time: 25 minutes

Instructor Notes:

1. Encourage students to identify inner choices (attitudes/beliefs) as well as outer choices (behaviors). One way to distinguish them is to point out that behaviors are visible, so they can be videotaped. Attitudes/beliefs are invisible, so they can't be videotaped.

2. In faculty development workshops that I conduct, I've asked thousands of college instructors which behaviors and attitudes/beliefs they consistently see in their successful students. Here are the top vote getters for behaviors: (1) attend class regularly, (2) do all assigned work and turn it in on time, and (3) participate actively. And instructors say the three crucial attitudes/beliefs are to (1) take personal responsibility, (2) be goal-directed, and (3) believe in yourself. Other beliefs high on the teachers' lists are "be self-disciplined, love learning, and have a positive attitude." You can inform students that all of these essential behaviors and attitudes are explored in *On Course*.

3. If there are any commitments that students choose unanimously, you could make these your course rules.

EXERCISE 1-3: Focus Questions

Purpose: To preview the course content and focus students' attention on finding answers to personally meaningful questions. Students also learn the power of using questions to find personally meaningful answers in readings, lectures, and class exercises/discussions.

Supplies and Setup: *On Course;* chalkboard (or blank overhead transparency); journal

Directions:

1. *Thumb through* On Course. *Examine the table of contents. Check out the summaries that precede each chapter. Look at the focus questions before each section of the text. Note the words in bold print in the text. Examine the diagrams, charts, cartoons, poems. Read some of the quotations in the margins. In your journal, jot down at least five questions that, if you discovered the answers to them during the semester, could affect your life for the better.* [5–10 minutes]

2. *Now, let's hear the questions you want answered. If you hear a question you'd like an answer to, add it to your list.* [Call for questions and record them for all to see. This process allows students to see the range of questions they could be finding answers for this semester.] [5–10 minutes]

3. *Put a star next to the five questions in your list that you most want answered. Your job this semester is to discover the answers to at least these five questions.*

Approximate Time: 10–20 minutes

Instructor Notes:

1. I find it best to record questions exactly as students give them to me.
2. Point out to students that every reading section begins with focus questions and that reading for the answers is one way to get the most from every assignment.
3. An option is to publish a class question list. For example . . .
   1. How can I manage my time better?
   2. Why do I feel so nervous when I take tests?
   3. How can I feel more confident?
   4. Why do I have to take this course?

When discussing the importance of questions in Journal #23, you can return to these questions and analyze which of them are Creator questions, which Victim questions.

EXERCISE 1-4: Relax

Purpose: To introduce students to the progressive relaxation method they will encounter in the introduction of *On Course.*

Supplies and Setup: You may wish to play music as you guide students through the relaxation. If so, you'll need a tape or CD player. Any instrumental music with a slow tempo (about 60 beats/minute) is fine. Environmental sounds (like the ocean or a babbling brook) also work well. Students often have favorite relaxation music you might want to ask them to bring in their music for future relaxation sessions.

Directions:
1. [If you wish, turn on the music or environmental sounds.] *We're now going to take a few minutes to relax. I'm simply going to read the progress relaxation* **Directions** *from* On Course *to familiarize you with the method presented in our book. Afterwards, we'll talk about your experience.* [Slowly read the directions for the Progressive Relaxation method from Chapter 1.] [5 minutes]
2. [Freewriting and/or Class Discussion] *What was the experience like for you? Do you feel any different now than you did before the relaxation? What's the life lesson here?* [e.g., When I take a few minutes to relax, I feel more energized.] [5–10 minutes]

Approximate Time: 10–15 minutes

Instructor Notes:
1. In the discussion, some students may express resistance to relaxing. I simply acknowledge what they say and move on without trying to change their minds. Only a positive personal experience with relaxation is likely to persuade students of its value. The goal of this exercise is to allow students to experience a relaxation method and share their honest experience. I find it most helpful to accept whatever their experience is without debate. Such acceptance begins to create a climate of trust in which all opinions are welcome and respected.
2. You might want to demonstrate how students can make a tape recording of the relaxation directions with music or environmental sounds in the background.

EXERCISE 1-5: Making Changes

Purpose: To identify specific changes students may wish to make in their lives.

Supplies and Setup: Students sitting in pairs (Student A and Student B). Students need their completed Journal Entry #1.

Directions:
1. *Student A, read to your partner what you wrote for Step 2 in Journal Entry #1 about your highest scores. Student B, when your partner finishes, tell him or her what you heard. Say, "What I hear you say is . . ." See how much you can remember. You'll have five minutes for reading and responding. Don't switch roles until I call time. If you finish early, take the time to get to know one another better.* [5 minutes]
2. *Now switch roles. B reads Step 2 to A. Then A responds, "What I heard you say is . . ." Again, you'll have five minutes for reading and responding.* [5 minutes]
3. *Student A, read to your partner what you wrote in Step 3 about your lowest scores. Student B, when your partner finishes, you'll say, "What I heard you say is . . ." Again, see how much you*

can remember. *You'll have five minutes for reading and responding. Don't switch roles until I call time.* [5 minutes]

4. *Now switch roles. B reads Step 3 to A. Then A responds, "What I heard you say is . . ." Again, you'll have five minutes.* [5 minutes]

5. [Freewriting and/or Class Discussion] *Now what's on your mind? As a result of what you learned in the self-assessment, are there any changes you'd like to make in yourself? What's the life lesson here?* [e.g., *It's amazing how much more I hear when I make a conscious effort to really listen.*] [5–10 minutes]

Approximate Time: 30–50 minutes

Instructor Notes:

1. This exercise is a powerful way to introduce the important issue of change. Points that might be made include: If you keep doing what you've been doing, you'll keep getting what you've been getting . . . Improving our lives requires change . . . Change can be threatening to some people . . . Change takes courage . . . The purpose of college is to help you change so you can improve your life.

2. If time allows, you might introduce this question: What might keep you from successfully making the changes you want to make?

3. Many teachers report the value of having students complete the self-assessment during class time. In this way you can better assure that students understand the directions and complete the questionnaire with a serious and purposeful attitude.

4. Students can also take the self-assessment on the Internet where they can immediately print out their results and, for comparison, the average scores of everyone else who has taken the self-assessment. To do so, visit the *On Course* website at *http://collegesurvival.college.hmco.com/students.*

Journal 2. Believing in Yourself: Develop Self-Acceptance

EXERCISE 2-1: What Is Self-Esteem?

Purpose: To identify the important contribution of self-esteem to success and to begin identifying choices for increasing self-esteem.

Supplies and Setup: Journals; students in groups of 3. Optional: Video of *Dead Poets Society;* VCR/TV monitor

Directions:

1. [Optional but recommended: Show the scene from *Dead Poets Society* in which the teacher (played by Robin Williams) has his students read poems that they wrote for homework. Stop the video after the scene in which the teacher asks a student named Todd to read and Todd says he didn't write a poem.] *How much do you suppose Todd believes in himself? How strong do you think Todd's self-esteem is? How can you tell? How successful do you think Todd will be in life if he doesn't increase his self-esteem? Why is strong self-esteem important to success?* [10 minutes]

2. *In your journal write your personal definition of self-esteem. You'll have an opportunity to revise your definition later if you wish.* [5 minutes]

3. *Read your definition of self-esteem to your group. Also, identify someone you know who has high self-esteem according to your definition.* [4–6 minutes]

4. *In your group, decide on three things a person can do to raise his or her self-esteem. Pick a group reporter to share your ideas with the class.* [5–10 minutes]
5. [Invite group reporters to tell each group's suggestions for raising self-esteem. Record suggestions on the chalkboard or on overhead transparency.] [5–10 minutes]
6. [Freewriting and/or Class Discussion] *Revise your definition of* self-esteem. *What do you think is the best way a person can raise his or her self-esteem? What's the life lesson here?* [e.g., I always thought that I was stuck with my self-esteem; now I feel hopeful that I can learn how to make it stronger.] [5–10 minutes]

Approximate Time: 35–45 minutes

Instructor Notes:
1. Here are five definitions of self-esteem that you could share with students to promote conversation:
    *   *Self-esteem is the ability to value one's self and to treat oneself with dignity, love, and reality.*—Virginia Satir
    *   *Self-esteem is the experience of being capable of managing life's challenges and being worthy of happiness.*—National Council for Self-Esteem
    *   *Self-esteem is the capacity to experience maximal self-love and joy whether or not you are successful at any point in your life.*—David Burns
    *   *Self-esteem is the feeling that we are worthwhile in our personal, social, and work lives. It comes from feeling loved and respected as a child in our family, by friends, and at school.*—Jeffrey E. Young and Janet S. Klosko
    *   *Self-esteem is the reputation we have with ourselves.*—Nathaniel Brandon

EXERCISE 2-2: Overheard Praise

Purpose: To expose students to the positive perceptions others have of them and to encourage them to begin accepting these positive qualities.

Supplies and Setup: Journals and pens; chime; students sitting in groups of 5 to 6. Chairs are in a small circle with one chair facing out from the circle. The students with their backs to the group have their journal open on their laps and pens in hand, ready to write.

Directions:
1. *Turn to the next clean page in your journal, and title the page "Overheard Praise." Keep your journal and pen with you throughout this exercise.* [1 minute]
2. *Notice that one person has his or her back to your group. Imagine that this person isn't there. In his or her absence, your group is going to talk about all the things you like and admire about that person. Since it's early in the semester, you probably don't know this person well yet, but you have probably noticed some positive qualities already. Whenever possible, recall specific events to explain what you're saying about the person. For example, I might say, "I admire Joe because he comes to class prepared." Or, "I like Joanne because she has the ability to see the best in everyone. Last week I heard her telling Robert what a good writer he is." While this conversation is going on, the person who is "absent" should be writing everything the other people say about him or her. Don't choose, just record everything. Each time I ring the chime, everyone moves one chair to the right. Then the group will begin talking about the new person whose back is to the group. Any questions? Okay, begin.* [4 minutes for directions; 2 minutes for the group to discuss each person] [15–20 minutes]

3. *Take a moment now to reread the overheard praise that you recorded in your journal. Let it sink in.* [2 minutes]
4. [Freewriting/Discussion] *What was that experience like for you? What was it like to give praise and appreciation? What was it like to hear praise and appreciation of you? Is it difficult or easy for you to accept the praise? How do you feel right now? What can you do to feel like this more often? What's the life lesson here?* [e.g., I'm going to be sure to give more praise to the people I love.] [10–20 minutes]

Approximate Time: 25–40 minutes

Instructor Notes:
1. Consider repeating this activity later in the course when students will have learned even more to praise one another.

CHAPTER 1: Quiz Questions

1. Taking the First Step

1. The quality of our lives is determined by the quality of the _____ we make on a daily basis.
2. When we choose positive beliefs, these lead to positive behaviors. Positive behaviors often lead to positive results that reinforce our positive beliefs, and the cycle begins anew. This sequence describes the cycle of _____.
3. A time-tested tool for designing the life you want to lead is a _____, a written record of your thoughts and feelings about your past, present, and future.
4. Five suggestions to help you create a meaningful journal are (1) be spontaneous; (2) write for yourself; (3) be honest; (4) be creative; and (5) _____.
5. When you relax and your brain waves slow down to 7–14 cycles per second, you have achieved _____ waves, which increase your learning capacity.

Answers: 1. choices   2. success   3. journal   4. dive deep   5. *alpha*

2. Believing in Yourself: Develop Self-Acceptance

1. Self-esteem is the reputation we have with others.   TRUE   FALSE
2. Self-esteem is strengthened by increased self-acceptance.   TRUE   FALSE
3. Accepting our weaknesses means _____.
   A. we are content to stay as we are
   B. we can now begin to change the things that can be changed
   C. we are weak
4. Successful people are usually willing to _____.
   A. admit their personal weaknesses
   B. set a goal to change
   C. manage their actions to bring about change
   D. look at feedback about their efforts to change
   E. have the courage to change
   F. do all of the above
5. We are born with a certain level of self-esteem, and it remains that way throughout our life. TRUE   FALSE

Answers: 1. FALSE (reputation with ourselves) 2. TRUE 3. B 4. F 5. FALSE (We can learn higher self-esteem just as we learned lower self-esteem.)

CHAPTER 1: Essay Topics

1. Many students come to college to be a "success," yet few have given great thought to what they mean by the term. In an essay written to your classmates in this course, offer your personal definition of success.
2. In a letter to a trusted friend, share with him or her what your self-assessment questionnaire revealed to be your greatest areas of strength and weakness.
3. Imagine that you have entered a writing contest for a college scholarship. The topic this year is to explain the changes that you want to make in yourself in order to be more successful in college and in life. Write this essay for the college scholarship committee.
4. Inform your teacher in this course about which of the eight choices of successful students will be the easiest for you to make and which will be the most difficult for you to make. Dive deep as you explain why.
5. Self-esteem is an important concept but one that is difficult to define. In an essay for a national magazine read by college students, write about a person you know who demonstrates high self-esteem. In this way, offer your readers your best definition of high self-esteem and how to achieve it.

Chapter 2
Accepting Personal Responsibility

Concept

There is great value in perceiving ourselves as the primary creator of the outcome of our lives. At the very least, we are responsible for how we respond to any event, whether the event is of our creation or not. When academic outcomes are negative, many students will blame others, often teachers. When academic outcomes are positive, many students will credit others. Since the cause of their results is seen as existing outside of themselves, these students have no reason to evaluate and possibly change their own behaviors. Students like this typically wait for the world to change while they complain, blame, make excuses, and repeat ineffective behaviors. By offering students the opportunity to see how their own choices contribute to their past, present, and future outcomes, we empower them to approach life with the beliefs and behaviors of a Creator, thus giving up the passivity and bitterness of a Victim.

Empowers Students to . . .

1. Accept the Creator role, taking responsibility for creating the outcome of their lives (including their education), AND to reject the Victim role, giving up complaining, blaming, and excusing.
2. Master Creator language, understanding that Creators and Victims choose different ways of thinking and speaking about their experience, consequently changing both their perception of reality and the outcomes that they create.
3. Live more consciously, becoming more aware of their inner aspects—Inner Critic, Inner Defender, and Inner Guide, among others—and the corresponding inner dialogue that dictates students' subsequent actions.
4. Make wise choices by consciously recognizing important decision points in their lives, identifying all possible options at this point, and making decisions with awareness of their future consequences.
5. Make mature decisions, choosing to make long-term gain more important than immediate pleasure or immediate escape from discomfort.
6. Replace outer authority with inner authority, and resistance with cooperation.
7. Gain greater control over the outcomes of their lives.

Remember to consider using the all-purpose exercises mentioned in the introduction, especially JOURNAL READINGS, QUOTATIONS, POEMS, CARTOONS, FOCUS QUESTIONS, AND CHAPTER-OPENING SUMMARIES. Remind students to use letters to label any in-class writing they do in their journals.

Journal 3.   Adopting the Creator Role ➤

EXERCISE 3-1: Responsibility Circle

Purpose: To become more conscious of how we create or contribute to many of the results that exist in our lives.

Supplies and Setup: Groups of 5 or 6 students sitting in a circle. Each student needs a pen and paper.

Directions:
1. *Write four statements that are true about you as a student (or other roles). Alternate between facts that you are happy with and facts that you are not happy with, for example: (1) I have a great schedule this semester. (2) My math teacher is boring. (3) My history teacher seems like a nice guy. (4) I'm not very motivated this semester. [5 minutes]*
2. *Start with the person who lives farthest from this room. Go clockwise around the circle, with each person reading his or her first statement, then around the circle again with each person reading the second statement, then a third time around, and so forth, until everyone has read all four statements. As you read your statement, add the following words: ". . . and I am responsible." For example, "I have a great schedule this semester, and I am responsible. My math teacher is boring, and I am responsible." Become conscious of how it feels to say that you are responsible for the situation with which you are happy or unhappy. [5 minutes]*
3. *[Freewriting/Group Discussion] Were there situations about which you said, "There's no way I'm responsible for this"? Were there situations about which you said, "Well, I guess I have to admit that I am at least partially responsible for that"? How do you decide what you are, in fact, responsible for in life? Would it be of any benefit to always assume that you are responsible for the results in your life? What's the life lesson here? [e.g., I have been blaming others for a situation in my life that I am actually more responsible for than I have wanted to admit.] [10–20 minutes]*

Approximate Time: 20–30 minutes

Instructor Notes:
1. Scott Peck, author of *The Road Less Traveled,* says that one of the most difficult things for human beings to decide is what they are and are not responsible for. Someone else (I don't recall who) has said that people who are neurotic take too much responsibility for the results in their lives, while people who are psychotic take too little responsibility. The challenge of being a Creator, then, is taking responsibility for the appropriate results in your life and not taking responsibility for the results that belong to others. Help students see that while they are certainly not responsible for all the results in their lives, they are, however, 100 percent responsible for how they respond to these results. If they always act as if they are responsible for the results in their lives, they will often discover life-improving choices for which they would not otherwise have even looked, let alone discovered.

EXERCISE 3-2: Victim/Creator Role-Play

Purpose: (1) To become familiar with the difference between how Creators and Victims respond to life's stimuli; (2) to see that we often have more options than we realize; and (3) to understand that each person responds sometimes as a Creator, sometimes as a Victim.

Supplies and Setup: 2 student volunteers (A & B). Role-playing is enhanced if students have already completed reading and writing Journal Entry #3.

Directions:
1. [To Student A] *Imagine that you work for B [student's name]. You're often late or absent. Today you arrived ten minutes late, and B confronts you. Because you're a great Victim, whatever B says to you, you'll respond by making excuses, blaming others, or complaining about something, like the employer's "unfair" rules. Whatever you do, don't accept any responsibility for your absence or lateness, and don't agree to try anything new.*
2. [To Student B] *You're the employer who has watched A often be late or absent. You're angry because A was 10 minutes late again today. Go ahead and role-play. As the angry employer, what would you say to A?*
3. *Let's repeat the same scene, except this time, A, you'll respond to your employer as a Creator instead of as a Victim.*
4. [Invite students to invent additional situations, especially in college, where some people respond as Victims. Repeat the role-play with as many situations as time allows.]
5. [Freewriting/Group Discussion] *How do Victims typically respond to life? How do Creators? Can you think of a time when you responded as a Victim? A Creator? Can you imagine the same person acting like a Victim in one situation and a Creator in another situation? What's the life lesson here?* [e.g., When I get upset, I tend to act more like a Victim than when I am feeling good.]

Approximate Time: About 10–12 minutes for each role-play and discussion

Instructor Notes:
1. An important point to bring out here is that a person is not solely a Victim or a Creator. We each have the capacity in any moment to respond as either. One key to success is to begin responding to life more often as a Creator.
2. After each role-play, you might say to the class, "Any suggestions on how the worker could be an even better Victim? An even better Creator?" Other students often want to try the same roles. Sometimes the original pair wishes a second take on the scene.

Journal 4. Mastering Creator Language

EXERCISE 4-1: The Language of Responsibility

Purpose: To practice language that supports responsible choices and to have an opportunity to meet a classmate.

Supplies and Setup: Handout of "Language of Responsibility" (next page). It's best if students have completed Journal Entry #4 before doing this activity.

Directions:
1. *Victims and Creators see the world very differently. As a result, they use different vocabularies to represent their realities. In other words, you can tell a Victim and a Creator by their choice of words. On the handout, translate the Victim language into Creator language. Keep in mind two qualities that characterize Creator Language. First, Creators accept ownership of their outcomes and experiences. Second, Creators plan and take specific actions to*

Language of Responsibility

Victim Talk	Creator Talk
1. I would be doing a lot better at this college if the teachers were better.	
2. They ought to do something about the food around here.	
3. I couldn't come to class because I had to go to the dentist for a checkup.	
4. You just can't pass a course when it's that hard.	
5. My boss makes me so angry.	
6. I can't help talking in class.	
7. I couldn't get the assignment because I was absent.	
8. I couldn't come to the conference I scheduled with you yesterday because my math teacher made me take a makeup test.	
9. People always get angry when they work hard and still fail a course.	
10. I couldn't attend class because I had to drive my mother to work.	
11. I would have called you, but my daughter got sick.	
12. They don't know what they're doing around here.	
13. I couldn't get to class on time because my last teacher kept us late.	
14. I tried calling him, but he's never home.	
15. I didn't have time to do my homework.	

improve their outcomes and experiences. So, you can recognize a Creator because they take ownership and action! [5–10 minutes]

2. [Class Discussion] *Okay, let's see what you came up with. Read one of the Victim statements, and give us your translation into Creator talk. Are there any you had trouble translating and you'd like to hear what someone else wrote?* [5–10 minutes]

3. [Journal Writing and/or Class Discussion] *Based on their different vocabularies, what would you say are the differences in the beliefs that Victims and Creators have about themselves? About other people? About the world? What do you think is the difference in the results created by Victims and Creators? What's the life lesson here?* [e.g., If I want to create my goals and dreams, I better learn to think and act more like a Creator and less like a Victim.] [5–10 minutes]

Approximate Time: 15–30 minutes

Instructor Notes:

1. Important concepts to come out in the discussion include: Victims believe that their behaviors, results, and feelings lie outside of them. They believe that other people and bad luck are responsible for their problems. As a result, Victims seldom achieve their goals and dreams. Creators more often—though not always—create their goals and dreams.

2. As you lead the discussion of the students' translations, reinforce the two qualities that characterize Creator Language: 1) ownership and 2) a plan of action.

EXERCISE 4-2: Have to/Choose to

Purpose: To demonstrate how language choices affect our attitude and our energy levels; to meet and interact with classmates.

Supplies and Setup: Journal

Directions:

1. *In your journal, draw a vertical line down the middle of a page. On the left side of the line, make a list of five things you "have to" do. Example: "**I have to** go to college"; "**I have to** call my mother on Sundays"; "**I have to** eat. . . ."* [3 minutes]

2. [Milling] *Everyone stand and choose a partner. Each partner reads from his or her list three things that he or she "has to" do. If you hear a new "have to" that is true for you, add it to your list. Then move on to a new partner and repeat the exchange of "have to's." Keep going until I call stop.* [5 minutes]

3. *Now, on the right side of the line, rewrite each of your sentences. Change "have to" to "choose to" and add a "because . . ." or "so . . ." clause to the sentence, one that gives a positive reason for your choice. Examples: "**I choose to** go to college because my degree will qualify me for the job I want"; "**I choose to** call my mother on Sundays so she will feel loved"; "**I choose to** eat because I want to be healthy."* [7 minutes]

4. [Milling] *Everyone stand and meet a partner as we did before. This time each of you will read three things that you "choose to" do. After you both read, move on to another partner. Keep going until I call stop. Notice if you feel any different this time.* [5 minutes]

5. [Freewriting and/or Group Discussion] *How did it feel to say "choose to" rather than "have to"? What does this experience suggest about how your language choices affect you? What is the life lesson here?* [e.g., I get myself upset by thinking I "have to" do something when the truth is

that I really *don't* have to do it. . . . I'm *choosing* to do it. Realizing this makes me feel a lot more in control of my life.] [5–10 minutes]

Approximate Time: About 20–30 minutes

Instructor Notes:

1. Remember, a great way to clarify directions is to give a demonstrate (DEMO). Steps 2 and 4 (above) will be most clear if you say, "So here's what that would look like . . ." and DEMO what you're asking for.

2. A point worth making in the discussion is that most people feel their energy level go up when they switch from "have to" to "choose to." That's because most people are depressed by Victim talk and energized by Creator talk.

Journal 5.   Making Wise Decisions

EXERCISE 5-1: The Wise-Choice Process

Purpose: To give students an opportunity to practice the Wise-Choice Process, a powerful tool of Creators.

Supplies and Setup: Journal #5 in *On Course* (students will need to refer to the six steps of the Wise-Choice Process); students in pairs

Directions:

1. *In your journal, briefly write about a current problem or difficulty in your life. It doesn't have to be a major problem. Choose a problem that you are comfortable talking about with the class.*

2. *Decide which partner will present a problem and which will be the Guide. The Guide will use the Wise-Choice Process to assist the other person to discover his or her best options.*

3. *Guide, ask your partner the six questions of the Wise-Choice Process. Your role is to guide your partner to discover his or her best options, not give advice. If you come up with an option your partner doesn't think of, you can always tell him or her after class. For this dialogue, offer no advice. The easiest way to do this is simple: **Stick to the six steps of the Wise-Choice Process.** Here's what that might look like. [DEMO the process.] Any questions? When you're ready, begin.*

4. *[Optional: If time allows, have partners switch roles and repeat Step 3.]*

5. *[Freewriting and/or Class Discussion] What was your experience as a Guide? How was it to avoid giving advice while helping your partner to solve his or her own problem? What was your experience as the person examining a problem? Did you discover positive options for solving your problem? What's the life lesson here? [e.g.,* By using the Wise-Choice Process, I came up with options that I had never thought of before.]

Approximate Time: 15 minutes for each time through the Wise-Choice Process; 5–15 minutes for discussion.

Instructor Notes:

1. An alternative format is to put students in trios instead of pairs. The third student acts as a silent observer during the Wise-Choice Process. Afterwards, the observer's role is to give feedback to the Guide about how well he or she followed the six steps of the Process. The observer's presence often causes the other two participants to focus more consciously on their

purpose—coming up with positive options, raising the quality of the results they create. If time allows, you can rotate the trio so each person has a chance to experience all three roles.

2. This process is very powerful. Students often say, "I didn't think this process would really work, but now that I've tried it, I see that it's a great tool for helping someone find positive options to solve a problem."

EXERCISE 5-2: The Road Not Taken

Purpose: To offer students an opportunity to see how their choices make all the difference in the outcomes of their lives.

Supplies and Setup: "The Road Not Taken" in *On Course* (p. 36)

Directions:

1. *I'd like a volunteer to read "The Road Not Taken" by Robert Frost.*
2. *The narrator of this poem came to a fork in the road: "Two roads diverged in a yellow wood." He had to take one road or the other, and he made a choice "that has made all the difference." In your journal, make a list of the major choice points you've faced in your life. For example, you might put "Attend college after high school or get a job." Or, "Get married or stay single." "Have a child or not." [5 minutes]*
3. *Let's hear some of your choice points. Just tell us your options, not what you chose. If you hear someone else mention a choice that reminds you of one you've made, add it to your list. [2–5 minutes, depending on the energy. A way to pick up the energy is to ask after a choice has been called out, "How many of you have also made a choice like this?"]*
4. *In the poem, Frost says, "Knowing how way leads on to way, I doubted if I should ever come back." Now pick one of your choices and go back to the moment of decision. In your journal, write about what your life would be like today if you'd taken the other road. For example, if one of your choice points was to marry or not, and you did marry, write what you imagine your life would be like today if you had not gotten married back then. [5 minutes]*
5. *Who'd be willing to read aloud what you wrote? How do you feel about that choice now that you've looked down the other road? Did you make a wise choice back then? What's the life lesson here? [Once I've made a decision, it's going to affect my life for years to come, so I better think it through before I make an important choice.] [3–5 minutes for each volunteer]*

Approximate Time: 15 minutes for Steps 1–4; 3–5 minutes for each volunteer in Step 5.

Instructor Notes:

1. The point here is threefold: to assist students to examine the wisdom of the previous choices they have made, to help them see that every choice they make impacts the quality of their future, and to show that all experiences contain life lessons if we look for them.
2. Listen for the Inner Critic badgering a student about a "bad choice." If a student is critical of his or her past choice, you might ask, "Is that your Inner Guide speaking or your Inner Critic?" If the student says, "That's my Inner Critic," you might respond, "Remember, your Inner Critic likes to wallow in what you did wrong while your Inner Guide takes ownership and then creates a plan to make things better. Which voice would be more helpful to listen to?" Most of all, resist giving advice to the student. Merely be a questioner and an active listener.

EXERCISE 5-3: Excuses/Reasons

Purpose: To consider the difference between mature reasons and immature excuses.

Supplies and Setup: Copies of the "Excuses/Reasons" (p. 16)

Directions:
1. *Rank the statements on the Excuses/Reasons sheet as explained in the **Directions**.* [5 minutes]
2. *Which statement did you rank #1 . . . as a Victim's excuse? Why?* [5 minutes]
3. *Which statement did you rank #9 . . . as a Creator's reasons? Why?* [5 minutes]
4. *[Journal Writing and/or Class Discussion] What differences do you see that distinguish Victims' excuses from Creators' reasons? What's the life lesson here?* [e.g., People love to pretend that their excuses are actually reasons, but pretending doesn't make that so.] [5–10 minutes]

Approximate Time: 20–25 minutes

Instructor Notes:
1. An important point to make in the discussion is that Victims tend to make choices that maximize immediate pleasure while harming future success. Creators don't allow themselves to get off course unless something of a much greater value comes along that needs their immediate attention, like rushing their child to the hospital because of an asthma attack.

Excuses/Reasons

Here are some choices that students have made more important than turning in a college assignment on time. Rank them from 1 through 9. Put a *1* next to the decision you consider to be merely a Victim's excuse. Put a *9* next to the decision you consider to be a Creator's reason. Rank the other decisions in order from 2 through 8, giving a different number to each statement.

Victim's Excuse 1 2 3 4 5 6 7 8 9 Creator's Reason

I didn't turn in my assignment on time because . . .

_____ I helped my aunt move to a new apartment.

_____ I rushed my daughter to the hospital because she was having an asthma attack.

_____ I stayed home to wait for the telephone repair man.

_____ I visited my boyfriend because he's having problems at home, and I felt like he needed me.

_____ I didn't look at my schedule carefully, so I totally forgot when the assignment was due.

_____ I had a headache and stayed home.

_____ I decided I could improve the assignment if I worked on it for a few more days.

_____ I started the assignment last night, and I didn't have time to finish it.

_____ I went to an appointment with another teacher instead of coming to class.

Case Study for Critical Thinking: The Late Paper

Purpose: To develop critical thinking skills by exploring a real-life situation that revolves around personal responsibility and the power of choices.

Supplies and Setup: "The Late Paper" in *On Course*

Directions:
1. [Have students read "The Late Paper." One way to be sure everyone has read the selection before taking the next step is to have one student read the first paragraph aloud, another student read the second, and so on until the reading is complete. Then have students put in their scores for the six characters.] [5 minutes]
2. [Find out by a show of hands how many students have picked each character as number one—most responsible for Kim's failing grade. If two or more characters are chosen as number one, move on to Step 3. In the unlikely event that everyone chooses the same character as number one (or there is otherwise little diversity in opinion), ask how many students have picked each character as number six—least responsible for Kim's failing grade. Often there is more diversity of opinion here.] [3 minutes]
3. [Create groups of like-minded students.] *Since you agree in your group about which character is most (or least) responsible for Kim's failing grade, decide how you are going to persuade other groups to agree with you. [5–10 minutes]*
4. [Have a spokesperson from each group present the group's position; then lead a debate on the issue by moving the discussion from group to group, allowing students to explain their positions in more detail and rebut opposing views. Invite students to demonstrate a change in their opinions by getting up and going to the group with which they now agree.] [5–20 minutes]
5. [Lead a discussion of the "Diving Deeper" question at the end of the case study.] [5–20 minutes]
6. [Journal Writing and/or Class Discussion] *What did you learn from this discussion about personal responsibility? What's the life lesson here? [e.g.,* Sometimes I have made blaming someone else take the place of doing what I needed to do in order to reach my goal.*] [5–10 minutes]*

Approximate Time: 25–55 minutes

Instructor Notes:
1. So as not to stifle discussion, I don't tell students what my scores are.
2. This class discussion is an excellent prewriting activity to be followed by students writing a persuasion essay supporting their choices for most or least responsible. Because students are now sharply aware of opposing views, they often write much more thorough and persuasive essays than would be the case without the debate.

Journal 6. Believing in Yourself: Change Your Inner Conversation

EXERCISE 6-1: Inner Dialogue Role-Play

Purpose: To dramatize the impact of the ongoing inner dialogue among the Inner Critic, Inner Defender, and Inner Guide.

Supplies and Setup: 4 volunteers (A, B, C, and D) for a role-play

Directions:
1. *Student A, you're going to speak to the class about your thoughts and feelings about college. There's no right or wrong thing to say, so just tell us whatever you want about your experience so far in college. Speak slowly.*
2. *Student B, you'll position yourself at Student A's right side and be his or her Inner Critic. This means that whatever Student A says, you'll find some way to criticize him or her for it. For example, if Student A says, "I like college," you might say, "You're a lousy math student; you can't even get to your classes on time . . ."*
3. *Student C, you'll position yourself at Student A's left side and be his or her Inner Defender. This means that whatever the Inner Critic says, you'll find some way to defend against the accusations by blaming problems on other people or circumstances. For example, you might say, "No one could be a good math student with such a lousy teacher. And with the terrible parking around here, of course you're late to your classes . . ."* [5–10 minutes]
4. [After the scene has played out] *So, Student A, what's on your mind right now? Did you recognize any of those voices? Do you think those voices have any effect on your success?* [Ask Inner Critic, Inner Defender, and class to add their observations.] [3–5 minutes]
5. *Now, Student D, you'll position yourself behind Student A and be his or her Inner Guide.* [It is effective if Student D is much taller than Student A—or stands on something to be above Student A.] *Your job is to offer a more objective view on Student A's life. For example, if the Inner Critic says, "You're a lousy math student," you might say, "You can improve your math skills by spending more time studying." If the Inner Defender says, "You have a lousy math teacher," you might say, "You can always go to the math lab to get additional help."* [3–5 minutes]
6. [Freewriting and/or Class Discussion] *So, what did you learn from this role-play? What's the life lesson here?* [e.g., I've got a lot of voices chattering in my head, and some of them won't help me achieve my goals. That's why it's really important that I am careful about which one I'm paying attention to.] [5–15 minutes]

Approximate Time: 25–40 minutes

Instructor Notes:
1. Let the role-play go for a long as it's entertaining and making a point. You'll probably have to slow down the dialogue, especially so that the Inner Guide has time to respond to the comments of the Inner Critic and Inner Defender. An important point to make is that the Inner Critic and the Inner Defender are inner voices of the Victim. The Inner Guide is the inner voice of the Creator. Our choice of which voices to listen to affects how we feel and what we do and, therefore, determines our results in life.

EXERCISE 6-2: Identifying Stinkin' Thinkin'

Purpose: To practice identifying irrational beliefs that tear away at our self-esteem.

Supplies and Setup: Students should have completed Journal Entry #6. Copies of the A + B = C chart (p. 19)

Directions:
1. *Fill in all the empty spaces in the A + B = C chart. Some items give you "A" (the Activating event) and "C" (the Consequence), and you must fill in "B" (the Belief). Others give you "A" and "B," and you must fill in "C." Still others give you only "A" and ask you to fill in both "B" and "C." Go ahead and do that now.* [10 minutes]

Activating Event + (What happened)	**B**elief(s) (What I think)	= Consequence (Emotions and behaviors)
1. I fail a midterm test.	1.	1. I get depressed and stop attending the course.
2. A friend doesn't meet me at the time we agreed upon.	2. My friend is usually very reliable and keeps his agreements.	2.
3. A speeding car cuts across two lanes of highway, just missing my car, then rockets off the next exit ramp.	3.	3.
4. Shortly after I hand in an essay, my instructor tells me, "I need to see you right away."	4.	4. I get very nervous and put off making an appointment to see my instructor.
5. I get an application for financial aid.	5. This form is very complicated, and I'm sure to make a mistake filling it out. I don't want anyone to know I'm confused.	5.
6. I'm going to be late for work for the third time this week. I've had one unexpected problem after another this week, but my employer doesn't know this, and she's bound to be furious when I get there.	6.	6.

2. [Lead a discussion about the Beliefs and Consequences the students have filled in for each event. For each item, ask:] *Is this belief wise thinkin' or stinkin' thinkin'? Is this event likely to raise or lower the person's self-esteem? What is the life lesson here?* [e.g., How I feel about myself depends more on what I believe than on what I accomplish.] [15–20 minutes]

Approximate Time: 25–30 minutes

Instructor Notes:
1. Remind students of psychologist Albert Ellis's belief that much of the world's emotional misery is caused by stinkin' thinkin', and stinkin' thinkin' leads to lowered self-esteem.
2. The important point to be made here is that any activating event allows for many possible responses. How we respond is a result of the core beliefs we hold about ourselves, other people, and the world, and it is these same core beliefs that powerfully affect our self-esteem.

CHAPTER 2: Quiz Questions

3. Adopting the Creator Role

1. When responsible people create the best life possible given their circumstances, they are acting as _____.
2. When irresponsible people allow life to happen to them, they are acting as _____.
3. The key ingredient of personal responsibility is _____.
4. When confronted by a stimulus, a Victim will typically _____.
5. When confronted by a stimulus, a Creator will usually _____.

Answers: 1. Creators 2. Victims 3. choice 4. complain (or blame, excuse, repeat behavior) 5. seek a solution (or take an action, try something new)

4. Mastering Creator Language

1. "My teacher is the cause of my problems" is something that would probably be said by your Inner _____.
2. "I'm so stupid, it's no surprise I failed math" is something that would probably be said by your Inner _____.
3. "I was thirty minutes late because the bus broke down" is something that would probably be said by your Inner _____. (Assume that the bus did break down but only for five minutes.)
4. "I was late because I chose to sleep thirty minutes later this morning" is something that would probably be said by your Inner _____.
5. "I don't think I'm smart enough to make it in college" is something that would probably be said by your Inner _____.

Answers: 1. Defender (blaming) 2. Critic (self-abusing) 3. Defender (excusing) 4. Guide (telling the objective truth) 5. Critic (self-abusing)

5. Making Wise Decisions

1. What we will experience in five or ten years is greatly affected by the choices we make from here on. TRUE FALSE
2. Your Inner Defender will be of great help as you take the first step of the Wise-Choice Process: What's my situation? TRUE FALSE

3. When you ask yourself, "Do I have a choice here?", the answer you always assume in the Wise-Choice Process is _____.
4. If you can't predict the outcome of one of your possible choices, you should stop and gather more information before making any decisions.   TRUE   FALSE
5. When people make a decision and begin acting on it, they typically feel more energized.   TRUE   FALSE

Answers: 1. TRUE 2. FALSE (Your Inner Guide will best help you define your present situation.)
3. "Yes" 4. TRUE 5. TRUE

6. Believing in Yourself: Change Your Inner Conversation

1. According to psychologist Albert Ellis, the following formula explains why people respond differently to the same event: A + B = C. In this formula, "A" stands for the activating event, and "C" stands for the consequence (how we feel about the activating event). What does "B" stand for? _____
2. "I'm stupid" is a typical comment made by an Inner _____.
3. "He's stupid" is a typical comment made by an Inner _____.
4. Disputing irrational beliefs is best done by the _____.
    A. Inner Critic
    B. Inner Defender
    C. Inner Guide
    D. Inner Tube
5. Being able to dispute irrational beliefs will help your self-esteem to grow.   TRUE   FALSE

Answers: 1. Belief(s) 2. Critic 3. Defender 4. C 5. TRUE

CHAPTER 2: Essay Topics

1. Many people who commit *ADD – What is the best test taking tip you read about* een wronged by society and that this justifies their crimes. Writ prison inmates about the differences between a Creator and a V
2. Some people have charged a continent of Victims: Whenever North Americans don't li argument goes, they blame others instead of taking persona gument for a newspaper editorial supporting or contradicting
3. Interview three or more i find out their opinion on how well students accept personal responsibility for their educations. Write an editorial for your college newspaper explaining what you discover.
4. Do most people use Victim language or Creator language? Take on the role of one who studies the way people use language. Go to a public place and listen to people talk. Write an article for a local magazine detailing what your research uncovers.
5. Psychologist Albert Ellis said that irrational beliefs (which he called "stinkin' thinkin") cause many of our problems. In an essay for your classmates, report on some of your own irrational beliefs that have gotten you off course and lowered your self-esteem. Offer rational beliefs that you could take on to dispute your stinkin' thinkin'.

Chapter 3
Discovering Self-Motivation

Concept

Choosing a meaningful purpose gives our lives a direction and creates inner motivation. Many students have not defined a personally meaningful purpose for being in college, let alone for being in a particular course. Unfocused, these students are more likely to drift **from** rather than **to** academic success. By offering them the opportunity to choose personally meaningful outcomes that they would like to achieve in college or in life, we assist students to create internal motivation and thus positively impact their persistence in the face of life's inevitable obstacles.

Empowers Students to . . .

1. Design a life plan that replaces external motivation with internal motivation.
2. Create a sense of "self" founded on their unique combination of personal roles, goals, and dreams.
3. Revise or upgrade their personal goals and dreams as a result of being exposed to the variety of aspirations held by other students.
4. Persist when they encounter obstacles that stand between them and their college education (or any other major goal).
5. Develop positive, affirming self-talk and powerful visualizations that will support them in pursuing their goals and dreams in the face of both internal and external obstacles.
6. Make and keep commitments to themselves.

Remember to consider using the all-purpose exercises mentioned in the introduction, especially JOURNAL READINGS, QUOTATIONS, POEMS, CARTOONS, FOCUS QUESTIONS, AND CHAPTER-OPENING SUMMARIES. Remind students to use letters to label any in-class writing they do in their journals.

Journal 7. Discovering Your Dreams

EXERCISE 7-1: Roles and Dreams

Purpose: To assist students to identify dreams that they have in their various life roles.

Supplies and Setup: A copy of the Roles and Dreams form (on page 23) for each student; students in pairs (A & B)

Directions:
1. *We each play many roles in life. A role is any function to which we regularly devote large chunks of time and energy. Write a list of your current roles, beginning with your role as "student." Continue your list with other roles that you play in your life; call them out as a reminder to others of their roles.*

Roles and Dreams

Role: _____
My dream:

Role: _____
My dream:

Role: _____
My dream:

Role: _____
My dream:

Role: _____
My dream:

Role: _____
My dream:

2. *Student A, you'll ask student B the following three questions, pausing after each for B to answer: "What is one of your roles? What do you want in this role? What experience are you looking for?" After you have asked the three questions once and they have been answered, ask them again; B can consider the same role or a different one. If B can't think of a desired outcome or experience in a role, ask, "What do you REALLY want in this role? What do you REALLY want to experience in this role?"*

3. *Student B, you'll respond each time to A's question. You can repeat the same role as many times as you want, but try to do all of your roles at least once. Any questions? Ready. Begin.* [A DEMO here will help illustrate the process. It helps to write the 3 questions on the chalkboard.] [5 minutes]

4. [After both partners have answered the questions aloud.] *Now fill in the boxes on your* Roles and Dreams *form. Identify your roles and what you really want—your dreams—in each role. What, for example, is your absolute biggest dream as a student? Is it a two-year associate's degree? A four-year bachelor's degree? A master's degree? A doctorate? Don't worry at this time about how you'll do it. What do you really want? Feel free to use words, pictures, symbols . . . whatever. It only has to make sense to you.* [5–10 minutes]

5. *Now we're going to do a walk-around. Take your* Roles and Dreams *form with you and meet someone. Introduce yourself; then tell one of your roles and a dream.* [DEMO by offering one of your own roles and dreams.] *After each of you has shared a role and dream, move on to another partner and do it again. No one owns a dream, so if you hear one you like, add it to your* Roles and Dreams *form. Make it your own!* [5–10 minutes, or as long as the energy in the room is high]

6. [Freewriting and/or Class Discussion] *What's on your mind right now about your dreams? What's the life lesson here?* [e.g., Thinking about my dreams gets me excited, so it's a great way for me to build my self-motivation.] [5–10 minutes]

Approximate Time: 20–30 minutes

Instructor Notes:
1. Giving a DEMO (demonstration) of what you want the students to do is essential in this (and in most) exercises. If you DEMO the process clearly, the students will move confidently and smoothly through it. Without a good DEMO, the activity often breaks down into confusion and requests for clarification.

EXERCISE 7-2: Guess My Dream

Purpose: To offer students an opportunity to re-evaluate their dreams, make a public statement of their dreams, and to hear the dreams of others.

Supplies and Setup: Guess My Dream (next page); pens; students in groups of 4 or 5

Directions:
1. *Finish the ten sentence stems on* Guess My Dream. [5–8 minutes]
2. *Decide who will go first in your group. Read sentences 1–9 to the group, but don't read sentence 10. After you read sentences 1–9, your group will have two minutes to guess what your dream is. After your group has guessed the dream or time runs out, read them sentence 10. I'll let you know when it's time to move on to the next person.* [5 minutes per person]
3. [Freewriting and/or Class Discussion] *What's on your mind right now about your dreams? What is the value of having dreams? Where do you suppose dreams come from? If you don't have a*

Guess My Dream

1. I really love to . . .

2. I'm very good at . . .

3. What I really want to have is . . .

4. What I really want to do is . . .

5. What I really want to be is . . .

6. Work that I would do even if I didn't get paid is . . .

7. After I'm gone, I want to be remembered for . . .

8. Someone I really admire for his or her achievements is . . .

9. The best compliment anyone can say to me is . . .

10. One of my biggest dreams is . . .

dream, how could you get one? What's the life lesson here? [e.g., Some people have a difficult time taking ownership of a big dream.] [5–10 minutes]

Approximate Time: 20–40 minutes

Instructor Notes:
1. Be sensitive to students who have yet to identify their dreams. Remind them that many successful people took years to find a dream that felt right to them. In the meantime, they set a goal to find a personally meaningful dream.
2. Remind everyone with a dream to stay open to an even more wonderful dream coming along.
3. Remind all students that one of the major values of having a personally meaningful dream is that it motivates us to do the difficult tasks that must be done to create success.

Journal 8.   Committing to Your Dreams

EXERCISE 8-1: Draw Your Dreams

Purpose: To assist students to visualize their dreams, thus creating greater commitment to the dreams.

Supplies and Setup: Dozens of felt-tip pens of various colors; journal books (or blank sheets of paper); students in groups of 3 to 5

Directions:
1. [Pass around the felt-tip pens, and ask students to take 3. Later, they can exchange with others if they want other colors.]
2. *Turn to the next clean page in your journal (or take out a blank sheet of paper). Using the colored markers, draw a picture or symbols of your greatest dream or dreams in life. You don't have to be a good artist; just use your imagination to create a picture of your dream.* [10 minutes]
3. *Each person in turn, show your drawing to your group and explain what your dream is. Be sure to (1) use present tense verbs, (2) be specific and concrete in describing your drawing, and (3) present it with the energy and emotion that it deserves. If you finish describing your dream before I indicate time to move on, the other members of your group can ask you questions about your dream. Each person will have four minutes.* [12–20 minutes, depending on group size]
4. [Freewriting and/or Class Discussion] *What is on your mind or heart after doing this activity? What's the life lesson here? [e.g.,* When people talk about their dreams in the present tense, they really describe them as if they already existed.] [5–10 minutes]

Approximate Time: 20–35 minutes

Instructor Notes:
1. Some Inner Critics will say, "But I can't draw. I'm no artist." Make it very clear that this is not an art contest. It is simply an opportunity to create a visual image of their dreams, something that they are all perfectly capable of doing.
2. Students will enjoy seeing your picture and hearing you explain it as well! Drawing your dream is powerful, and I urge you to get some of the power for yourself. I have pictures of my dreams framed and hanging in my bedroom for inspiration.
3. If you have a student with a particularly powerful dream, consider videotaping him or her explaining it, and use the tape to inspire future classes.

EXERCISE 8-2: I Have a Dream

Purpose: To offer students an illustration of the motivating power of commitment to a dream.

Supplies and Setup: Video of Martin Luther King's "I Have a Dream" speech. Most likely your college library has (or can get) a copy.

Directions:
1. *I'd like to introduce you to someone who had one of the most motivating dreams of the twentieth century.* [Show all or part of "I Have a Dream." The last 6 or 7 minutes are particularly stirring.] [6–15 minutes]
2. [Freewriting and/or Class Discussion] *What's on your mind or heart after hearing Dr. King's dream? How committed do you suppose Dr. King was to his dream? How do you suppose he developed such a commitment to his dream? What did his dream motivate him to do? What difference do you suppose Martin Luther King's dream made in the quality of his life? If you have a dream, how committed are you to its fulfillment? How do you suppose you could strengthen your commitment? What difference would increasing your commitment to your dream make to your life? What's the life lesson here?* [e.g., Dreams give you the courage to make difficult choices.] [10–20 minutes]

Approximate Time: 15–30 minutes

Instructor Notes:
1. I have watched this speech many times, and it never fails to move me. I believe I'm affected most by the realization that Dr. King had such a commitment to his dream that he was motivated to present it to a quarter of a million people at the Lincoln Memorial and to millions more on film. Dr. King's example causes me to ask myself, "What dream do I have about which I feel that much passion and commitment?"

Journal 9.   Designing a Compelling Life Plan

EXERCISE 9-1: Looking Back

Purpose: To offer students an opportunity to consider the quality of their present life plan.

Supplies and Setup: Journals; students in pairs (A & B). Have students exchange journals.

Directions:
1. *Partner A, imagine that it is many years from now and you are close to the end of your life. Partner B has come to visit you in the last few days of your life. Partner B will ask, "Have you had a rich and personally fulfilling life?" Partner A, answer "Yes" or "No" and then tell your partner why. Partner B, write your partner's reasons in his or her journal. Any questions? If not, begin with Partner B asking, "Have you had a rich and personally fulfilling life?"* [5 minutes]
2. *Now, Partner B will ask the same question. Only this time, Partner A, give the opposite answer. For example, if you said "Yes" before, now say "No, I have not had a rich and personally fulfilling life." Then go on to explain why. Once again, Partner B will record your reasons. Any questions? If not, begin. Partner B, ask your friend, "Have you had a rich and personally fulfilling life?"* [5 minutes]
3. [Reverse roles and repeat Steps 1 and 2.] [10 minutes]
4. *Exchange journals and read over the lists that your partner has recorded for you.*

5. [Journal Writing and/or Class Discussion] *What is on your mind? In your heart? What did you learn by doing this exercise? Are there any changes you want to make in your life plan? What's the life lesson here?* [e.g., Many people probably die without having done much more than talk about their dreams. I'm not going to let that happen to me.] [5–15 minutes]

Approximate Time: 25–40 minutes

Source: Jessica Dibb, Inspiration Seminars

Instructor Notes:
1. If possible, it is effective to have the "dying" partner lying down.

EXERCISE 9-2: Eulogy for Myself

Purpose: To offer students an opportunity to consider the quality of their present life plan.

Supplies and Setup: Paper and pens for each student

Directions:
1. *Imagine that you have died. The person who knows you best in life undertakes the task of delivering the eulogy at your funeral. Write the eulogy this person would deliver. Write it neatly enough that someone else can read it. Do not put your name on it.* [10 minutes]
2. [Collect all the eulogies and redistribute them so that no one knows whose eulogy he or she has.]
3. *I'd like a volunteer to come up front and read the eulogy that you have.* [Have as many eulogies read as you have time for. 2–3 minutes each]
4. [Journal Writing and/or Class Discussion] *How did you feel during this activity? What did you learn from writing and listening to the eulogies? Are there any changes you want to make now in your life plan? What's the life lesson here?* [e.g., I'm not going to live forever, so I better start taking steps to make my life something I'll be proud of.] [5–15 minutes]

Approximate Time: 20–45 minutes

Instructor Notes:
1. After a eulogy is ready, you can have students try to guess whose it is, explaining their choices. Then the true author of the eulogy can identify himself or herself or not.
2. A time-saving alternative is to have students write one sentence they would like carved on their gravestone.

Case Study for Critical Thinking: Popson's Dilemma

Purpose: To develop critical thinking skills by exploring a real-life situation that revolves around self-motivation.

Supplies and Setup: "Popson's Dilemma" in *On Course*

Directions:
1. [Have students read "Popson's Dilemma." One way to be sure everyone has read the selection before taking the next step is to have one student read the first paragraph aloud, another student read the second, and so on until the reading is complete. Then have students put in their scores for the eight professors.] [5 minutes]

2. [Find out by a show of hands how many students have picked each professor as number one—the best advice for motivating Professor Popson's student. If two or more characters are chosen as number one, move on to Step 3. In the unlikely event that everyone chooses the same character as number one (or there is otherwise little diversity in opinion), ask how many students have picked each character as number eight—worst advice for motivating Professor Popson's student. Often there is more diversity of opinion here.] [3 minutes]
3. [Create groups of like-minded students.] *Since you agree in your group about whose advice is best (or worst) for motivating Professor Popson's student, decide how you are going to persuade other groups to agree with you.* [5–10 minutes]
4. [Have a spokesperson from each group present the group's position; then lead a debate on the issue by moving the discussion from group to group, allowing students to explain their positions in more detail and rebut opposing views. Invite students to demonstrate a change in their opinions by getting up and going to the group with which they now agree.] [5–20 minutes]
5. [Lead a discussion of the "Diving Deeper" question at the end of the case study.] [5–20 minutes]
6. [Journal Writing and/or Class Discussion] *What did you learn from this discussion about self-motivation? What motivates you? If like the student in the case study, you begin to lose your motivation in college, what could you do to get it back? What's the life lesson here?* [e.g., No one else can really motivate us; we're each responsible for creating our own motivation.] [5–10 minutes]

Approximate Time: 25–55 minutes

Instructor Notes:
1. So as not to stifle discussion, I don't tell students what my scores are.
2. This class discussion is an excellent prewriting activity to be followed by students writing a persuasion essay supporting their opinion in the debate. Because students are now sharply aware of opposing views, they often write much more thorough and persuasive essays than would be the case without the debate.

Journal 10.   Believing in Yourself: Write a Personal Affirmation

EXERCISE 10-1: Revising Toxic Messages

Purpose: To demonstrate how affirmations can dispute the toxic messages of the Inner Critic.

Supplies and Setup: Journals; students in pairs (A & B)

Directions:
1. *Draw a line down the middle of the next clean page in your journal.*
2. *What you are about to write will NOT be shared with anyone. On the left-hand side of the page, I'd like you to write any criticisms you can ever recall hearing from significant adults in your life. Skip a line after each one. For example, maybe your mother once told you, "You're the most selfish child I've ever known." Or your father told you, "You're the laziest child in the world." Or your teacher told you, "Your writing is poor."* [Pause as they write.] *What criticisms do you recall about your thinking ability? . . . Your emotions? . . . Your body? . . . Your school-work? . . . Your physical abilities? . . . The kind of person you are? . . .* [5 minutes]
3. *What you are about to write WILL be shared with others. Now, write in the right-hand column a positive statement that reclaims the quality that you were criticized for. For example, if the*

criticism is "You're lazy," you'd counter with "I am a hard worker." If the criticism is "You're stupid," you'd counter with "I am intelligent." [5 minutes]

4. *Partner A, read only your positive statements to Partner B. Partner B, listen carefully, and when your partner is done, tell your partner what you heard: "I heard you say that you are a hard worker and you are intelligent."* [2–4 minutes, based on the energy level of the room]

5. *Now reverse roles. Partner B, you read your positive statements, and Partner A, you say what you heard.* [2–4 minutes]

6. [Freewriting and/or Class Discussion] *What is on your mind? In your heart? What did it feel like to say those positive statements? What did it feel like to listen to your partner's positive statements? How have the negative voices in your head hindered you in the past? How would your life be different if you heard the positive statements more? What's the life lesson here?* [e.g., If I refuse to allow negative thoughts to spend time in my mind, I'll feel a lot better about myself, and I'll probably get a lot more done, too.] [5–15 minutes]

Approximate Time: 20–35 minutes

Instructor Notes:
1. This activity makes a great setup for the affirmation writing process in Journal #10.

EXERCISE 10-2: Affirmation Milling

Purpose: To take ownership of one's personal affirmation and hear other people's affirmations. This activity also builds a sense of community in the classroom.

Supplies and Setup: 3" x 5" cards, 2 per student. Students need to have already completed Journal Entry #10, having written their personal affirmations.

Directions:
1. *Open your journals to the page where you wrote your affirmations for Journal #10. Make two copies of your affirmation on the 3" x 5" cards.*

2. *Now we're going to get up, walk around the room, and greet other people in the room with our name and our affirmations. You can take your cards if you want.*

3. *Here's what it will look like: You'll walk up to someone like this.* [DEMO this by actually going up to a student.] *Then you'll shake hands and say your name and affirmation like this: "Hi, my name is Skip, and I am a bold, happy, loving man." Your partner will respond, "Yes, you are!" And you reply, "I know!"* [Encourage the student you're demonstrating with to say that to you.] *Now your partner will say his or her name and affirmation, and you'll respond, "Yes, you are!", and your partner will reply, "I know!"* [Encourage the student you're DEMOing with to say his or her affirmation, and you respond with a rousing "Yes, you are!" Ham it up and be lighthearted!] [2 minutes]

4. *Okay, let's do it. And have fun! Keep meeting people with your affirmation until I call stop.* [4–6 minutes]

5. [Freewriting and/or Class Discussion] *How do you feel right now? What's on your mind? Were you aware of any voices in your head while you were doing it? What were they saying? Whose voices were they? When would be great times to say your affirmation to yourself? What's the life lesson here?* [e.g., The more I say positive things about myself, the more I believe them, and when I believe them, I start acting like they are true.]

Approximate Time: 10–20 minutes

Instructor Notes:

1. The messages students often hear in their heads while doing this activity are "I feel stupid doing this" or "Others will think I'm weird." This is the voice of the Inner Critic. Other messages might include "The teacher is stupid for making us do this" or "This activity is the dumbest thing I've ever experienced." This is the voice of the Inner Defender. Help students acknowledge these voices without judgment so they can begin to hear the more supportive voices of their Inner Guides in their affirmations.

2. Very rarely (in my experience) a student will not want to share his or her affirmation with classmates. (Some cultures, for example, frown on saying such positive things about oneself.) Remind students that they can always pass on doing an exercise.

3. I collect one card with the students' affirmations from each student. On my laser printer, I print the affirmations on certificates or paper frames (available from office supply stores) and give them out at the next class. Students love to get this official-looking copy of their affirmation!

CHAPTER 3: Quiz Questions

7. Discovering Your Dreams

1. A **life role** is any function to which we regularly devote large amounts of _____ and energy.
2. Having a dream creates motivation and energy. TRUE FALSE
3. A dream that expresses what you truly value guides the _____ that you make every day.
4. Once you choose a dream, you should never change it. TRUE FALSE
5. If you discover a dream that doesn't fit into any of your current roles, you should _____.
    A. give up the dream
    B. change majors in college
    C. create a new life role

Answers: 1. time 2. TRUE 3. choices 4. FALSE 5. C

8. Committing to Your Dreams

1. When people doubt they are good enough to achieve dreams that they are actually quite capable of achieving, they are listening to the voice of their _____.
    A. Inner Critic
    B. Inner Defender
    C. Inner Guide
2. A(n) _____ is an unbending intention, a decision that you are unwilling to change despite setbacks.
3. All of our accomplishments are created twice. Before we can create them in the world, we need to create them first in our _____.
4. Which of the following is NOT a key to effective visualizing? _____
    A. Relaxing
    B. Using present tense verbs
    C. Being specific
    D. Feeling your feelings
    E. Humming softly

5. Keeping your commitment may be even more important than actually achieving your dream because when you are on course to a personally meaningful dream, you will learn and grow in ways that you cannot imagine today.   TRUE   FALSE

Answers: 1. A   2. commitment   3. minds   4. E.   5. TRUE

9. Designing a Compelling Life Plan

1. A short-term goal is a steppingstone to accomplishing a _____.
2. A long-term goal is a steppingstone to accomplishing a _____.
3. According to psychologist Brian Tracy, people don't set goals because (1) they don't realize the importance of goals, and (2) they don't know how to set goals.   TRUE   FALSE
4. The DAPPS Rule is a memory device to assist us in remembering the five qualities of an effective _____.
5. The five letters in DAPPS stand for _____, _____, _____, _____, and _____.

Answers: 1. long-term goal   2. dream   3. TRUE   4. goal   5. dated, achievable, personal, positive, specific

10. Believing in Yourself: Write a Personal Affirmation

1. We must depend on others to tell us what we should believe about ourselves.   TRUE   FALSE
2. A personal _____ is a statement about ourselves in which we claim our desired qualities as if we already had them in abundance.
3. If someone's Inner Critic keeps saying, "I am dumb," that person can create an affirmation that says _____.
4. If you want to strengthen your affirmation, which of the following would you NOT do? _____
   A. Realize that you already possess the qualities you desire.
   B. Heed your Inner Critic.
   C. Repeat your affirmation over and over.
   D. Say your affirmation while looking in the mirror.
5. If you want to further strengthen your affirmation, which of the following would you NOT do? _____
   A. Criticize other people before they criticize you.
   B. Be vigilant about all the other words you use to describe yourself.
   C. Say your affirmation when life tests you.
   D. Record your affirmation on a 3-minute loop tape and listen to it often.

Answers: 1. FALSE   2. affirmation   3. I am smart (or a similar affirmation of intelligence) 4. B   5. A.

CHAPTER 3: Essay Topics

1. Many students are unsuccessful in college because they don't see how college is going to help them create the life they want to live. Write an essay in which you define both what you want to accomplish in your life and how college is going to be an important steppingstone to that success.

2. Some critics suggest that today's college students have no sense of commitment to causes bigger than themselves. If this is an unfair criticism of you as a college student, write a letter to the editor of your local newspaper in which you define exactly what important cause(s) you feel committed to and why.

3. The ability to have a clear picture of the future you want to create is a great help in creating it. Write an essay in which you describe in detail what you would like to have, do, and be twenty years from now.

4. Personal affirmations are helpful for countering the negative self-talk of our Inner Critic. Write an essay in which you explore what messages you consistently get from your Inner Critic, where you think you got them from, and the kind of self-talk that you plan to engage in to minimize the damage your self-judgments will have on your success.

5. Some people find it extremely difficult to identify their personal goals and dreams. If this is true for you, write a formal letter to your teacher describing your lack of goals and dreams, speculate on why this is so, explain how you feel about it, and suggest what, if anything, you plan to do about this situation.

Chapter 4
Mastering Self-Management

Concept

Most major life goals are achieved by taking purposeful actions consistently over time. Raised in a culture that relishes instant gratification, many students have not learned the rewards of taking persistent, small steps toward a distant personal goal. Without an effective action plan, many students fail to initiate the steps that they are perfectly capable of taking to achieve their goals. By regularly offering them an opportunity to choose their next action steps and by acknowledging them for taking these actions (regardless of the outcome), we help students to experience the benefit of taking persistent, purposeful actions.

Empowers Students to . . .

1. Live life actively, rather than passive, understanding that the key to effectiveness is not time management but self-management.
2. Choose, prioritize, and schedule purposeful actions that will move them toward their goals and dreams.
3. Use written tools of self-management. (monthly planners, next actions lists, 32-day commitments, tracking forms) to get and stay on course.
4. Use effective tracking tools to make necessary course corrections.
5. Replace compliance with or defiance against outer rules with cooperation with inner rules that, over time, develop into supportive habits.
6. Develop self-discipline, including the abilities to focus and to persist in the face of obstacles.
7. Raise personal standards about the quality of work they do.
8. Visualize themselves successfully doing purposeful actions.

Remember to consider using the all-purpose exercises mentioned in the introduction, especially JOURNAL READINGS, QUOTATIONS, POEMS, CARTOONS, FOCUS QUESTIONS, AND CHAPTER-OPENING SUMMARIES. Remind students to use letters to label any in-class writing they do in their journals.

Journal 11. Acting on Purpose

EXERCISE 11-1: Time Wasters

Purpose: To raise students' consciousness about how they waste time in Quadrants III and IV and to offer students an opportunity to experience a week where they consciously avoid one of these unpurposeful behaviors.

Supplies and Setup: Students in groups of 5. One person in each group needs pen and paper. Write the following on the chalkboard (or put on overhead transparency): **I waste time by . . .**

Directions:

1. *Decide who will be your group's recorder. That person needs a pen and paper. The person to the left of your recorder will go first. That person will complete the following sentence stem: "I waste time by . . ." Going clockwise, the next person will complete the sentence again. Keep going around and around until I say stop. It's perfectly okay to repeat what someone else has said, but try not to repeat yourself. The recorder will make a list of all the different ways that people in your group waste time.* [5 minutes]

2. *Let's hear from the recorder in each group. What are the top three ways people in your group waste time?* [You may want to record the responses on the chalkboard or an overhead transparency. Continue with all groups.] [5–10 minutes, depending on number of groups]

3. [Freewriting and/or Class Discussion] *What did you learn from this exchange of ideas? What Quadrant III and IV actions are habits of yours? What's the life lesson here?* [e.g., When I'm not working on a goal that is important to me, I waste a lot of time.] [5–15 minutes]

4. *I'd like to invite you to try an experiment this week, an experiment that could change the quality of your life. The experiment is to say "No" to one Quadrant III or Quadrant IV action that is a habit of yours. Keeping this commitment will free up time for actions in Quadrants I and II. Remember, this is for just one week. After that you can decide if you want to stop completely. So, who'd be willing to make the commitment to yourself to give up one unpurposeful action for a week?* [You may wish to keep a record of the commitments and follow up on them in subsequent classes.] [5–10 minutes]

Approximate Time: 20–35 minutes

Instructor Notes:

1. Make sure students are clear about the kinds of behaviors that occur in each of the four quadrants: Quadrant I (Important and Urgent), Quadrant II (Important and Not Urgent), Quadrant III (Unimportant and Urgent), Quadrant IV (Unimportant and Not Urgent).

EXERCISE 11-2: Who Wants This Prize?

Purpose: To demonstrate that wanting something is not enough; one also has to take purposeful actions.

Supplies and Setup: A prize of value to your students. (A sure bet is a dollar bill, but you can probably be more creative than that . . . perhaps a popular book or CD.)

Directions:

1. [Hold up the prize.] *I have a prize here.* [Describe it, making it very desirable.] *Who would like it?* [Keep asking the question until someone comes up and takes it from you or until a few minutes go by.] [3–4 minutes]

2. [Freewriting and/or Class Discussion] *How many of you wanted the prize? Who got it? What did he or she do that no one else did? What is the life lesson here?* [e.g., It's not enough to just want something; you have to take positive actions or you won't get it.] [5–10 minutes]

3. [In preparation for our later consideration of rules, valuable groundwork can be laid and an interesting discussion begun with the following questions.] *For all of you who didn't come forward to take the prize, what messages do you have in your heads that stopped you? Where*

did you get these rules? In what circumstances will these rules help you? Hinder you? What's the life lesson here? [*e.g.,* Some of the things I believe are the very things that will keep me from taking the actions I need to take to succeed.] [5–10 minutes]

Approximate Time: 10–25 minutes

Journal 12. Employing Self-Management Tools

EXERCISE 12-1: Rocks and Sugar

Purpose: To demonstrate the value of doing purposeful actions first.

Supplies and Setup: 2 one-quart glass jars, 1 empty, 1 about three-fourths full of sugar; enough irregularly shaped rocks to nearly fill the empty glass jar

Directions:
1. *We're going to imagine that this empty glass jar is a day in your life. The sugar represents unimportant actions: Quadrant III and IV actions. They are sweet at the moment, but they don't move us toward our goals and dreams. They provide instant gratification with no long-term benefit. What would be some examples of these low-priority actions?* [Talking for hours on the phone, watching TV, excessive partying.] *These rocks represent your important actions: Quadrant I and II actions. Important actions move us steadily toward our goals and dreams. Important actions build a strong foundation for success. What would be some examples of important actions?* [Studying for a test, going to classes, applying for a job, exercising]
2. *Now I'm going to pour the sugar into this empty jar which—keep in mind—represents a day in your life. So on this day, you're choosing to do unimportant actions first. Now, I'm going to add the rocks, which represent your important actions. What do you notice?* [Very few of the rocks will fit in the jar.]
3. *Now, we'll do it a different way. First, I'll put all the rocks into the empty jar. This represents choosing to do your purposeful actions first. Now, I'm going to pour the sugar into the jar after the rocks. What do you notice this time?* [The sugar fills in between the rocks, and much, perhaps all, of the sugar will go into the jar.] [5 minutes for the whole demonstration]
4. [Freewriting and/or Class Discussion] *What is the life lesson in the rocks and sugar demonstration?* [When you do your important tasks first, you can put more into each day.] [5–10 minutes]

Approximate Time: 10–15 minutes

Instructor Notes:
1. The key to a successful demonstration is having rocks that are so irregular that they do not sit tight against one another in the jar, thus leaving room for the sugar to settle in between them.
2. Worth stressing: We can't manage time, but we can manage our own actions. The key is making wise choices. Doing important actions first is a wise choice.

EXERCISE 12-2: Time Savers

Purpose: To discover specific strategies for making the most of every twenty-four hours.

Supplies and Setup: Groups of 4 to 5. The group recorder needs a pen and paper.

Directions:

1. *Almost everyone has developed strategies for saving time. In your group, have a discussion of your best ideas for saving time, and have one person record each suggestion. Here are a few examples:*

   • *I record my favorite television shows on my VCR and watch them later at night when I'm too tired to study. Also, I can fast-forward through the commercials, allowing me to watch an hour show in about forty minutes. I figure this saves me at least two hours each week.*

   • *I carry a list of telephone calls that I have to make. Any time I have a few minutes, I pull out my list and make a call. I figure this saves me at least an hour each week.*

   • *On Sundays I cook large batches of food and freeze them in sizes just right for one meal. During the week, I pull out a frozen meal, heat it, and eat. I figure this saves me about three to four hours per week. This strategy saves me money as well as time because, with meals already prepared, I'm much less inclined to go out to eat.*

   So, your job is to come up with a list of great ways to save time. Any questions? Okay, begin. [5–10 minutes]

2. *Now let's have the recorder report each group's best ideas.* [You may want to write them on the chalkboard or on an overhead transparency.] [5–10 minutes]

3. [Freewriting/Discussion] *Which of these time savers will you try this week? What's the life lesson here?* [e.g., I may not be able to add hours to a day, but I can take actions that will make it seem like I have more time.] [5–15 minutes]

Approximate Time: 20–30 minutes

Instructor Notes:

1. Worth stressing: We can't manage time, but we can manage our own actions. The key is making wise choices.

Journal 13. Developing Self-Discipline

EXERCISE 13-1: Focused Hands

Purpose: To demonstrate the importance of staying focused on the task at hand.

Supplies and Setup: Pairs of students (A & B) standing facing one another.

Directions:

1. *Place your hands in front of you, palms facing and about one inch from your partner's but not touching. Partner A, your job is to move your hands up, down, back, forward, any way you want (but you can't move your feet). Partner B, your job is to follow your partner's hands, always keeping your palms about one inch from your partner's palms. Your hands should never touch.* [DEMO the process with a student.] *Any questions? Okay, go.* [2 minutes]

2. *What did you notice?* [3 minutes]

3. [Switch roles and repeat Steps 1 and 2.] [5 minutes]

4. [Freewriting and/or Class Discussion] *What's the life lesson here?* [Almost always someone will write or express the idea of "focus." With that comment as a transition, lead the discussion to an in-depth consideration of "focus" with questions like these: What happened when you lost focus on your goal? What caused you to lose focus? How did you regain focus? Have you ever lost focus in your life? What happened? How strong is your focus right now on college? What could you do to strengthen your focus?] [5–15 minutes]

Approximate Time: 10–25 minutes

Source: Various presenters. The first time I saw this exercise, it was led by David Ellis.

EXERCISE 13-2: The Graduation Game

Purpose: To demonstrate that graduation and other life successes are usually the result of student's taking small, purposeful actions persistently over time. This activity takes a bit more setup than most in this manual, but it's well worth it. Students will be talking about 3-foot tosses the rest of the semester.

Supplies and Setup: Ring toss set (use 1 post and 3–6 rings); tape on the floor marking 30 feet at 3-foot intervals; chalkboard or a transparency.

Directions:
1. *Today we're going to play The Graduation Game. This game teaches an important lesson about HOW to earn a college degree or accomplish any important goal or dream.*
2. *I need 6 volunteers to play.* [You can play with any number from 2–30, but the more players there are, the longer the game takes.]
3. *Every player has the same goal in this game—to graduate as quickly as possible.*
4. *In this game, you graduate when you earn 30 or more credits.*
5. *You earn credits by making a ringer. Each ringer earns credits equal to the distance thrown, and you can throw from any distance you choose. For example, a ringer from 6 feet earns 6 credits; a ringer from 24 feet earns 24 credits, and so on. You can throw from the same distance every time or you can change the distance from which you throw every time . . . it's your choice.*
6. *Everyone playing will take turns tossing the rings until someone earns 30 or more credits and graduates. Before you toss each time, write on the board [or transparency] the number representing the distance from which you'll toss. After you toss, circle the number if you get a ringer. When your score totals 30 or more credits, shout "I graduate!"* [When someone gets 30 or more credits and "graduates," allow everyone to complete the same number of tosses, then stop the game.]
7. [Freewriting and/or Discussion] *So, what lesson does the ring toss game teach us about being successful in college?* [e.g., Life is a breeze in persistent 3-foot tosses...Life is hard by the yard but a cinch by the inch...You can eat a whale if you do it one bite at a time...You have to climb a mountain one step at a time.] *What would a 30-foot toss look like in college?* [e.g., Not studying all semester, then cramming the night before an exam; taking 20 credits in 1 semester while working full-time.] *What would a 3-foot toss look like in college?* [e.g., Coming to every class; handing in every assignment when due; asking questions when you have them.] [Some students will argue that 3-foot tosses are no challenge and that it's more exciting to take longer tosses. In the likely event that the person who graduated first took many 3-foot tosses, point that out. Remind them that they have every right to choose the excitement of a 30-foot toss, but it might be at the expense of achieving their goals or dreams.] *Now let's apply this lesson to the rest of our lives: In life, what distance do you typically toss from? Are you a 30-foot tosser, a 15-foot tosser, a 3-foot tosser? Are you happy with the outcomes and experiences you've been creating this way? Are there any changes you plan to make in the way you pursue your goals and dreams? Do you have any large projects that would benefit from being broken into persistent 3-foot tosses?*

Approximate Time: 30–55 minutes, depending most on the length of discussion

Source: This is a variation on a demonstration I first saw done by Ron and Mary Hulnick at the University of Santa Monica.

Instructor Notes:
1. In my experience, the person with the most 3-foot tosses almost always wins, but even if another person wins, you can make the point that sometimes someone wins the lottery, too. The fact remains that most of the time, 3-foot tosses lead to success, so it still comes down to a choice of which way we will pursue our goals and dreams. Do you want to trust your future success to 30-foot tosses or 3-foot tosses?
2. This game creates a powerful metaphor to which you can return over and over. When someone is pondering an action to take toward her goal, you can say, "So what would a 3-foot toss look like in this situation?" or "That sounds like a 30-foot toss to me. Could you break that into smaller, 3-foot tosses?
3. I ask players to say their name and affirmation before tossing the ring. In the process, class-mates learn one another's names and affirmations.

Case Study for Critical Thinking: The Procrastinators

Purpose: To develop critical thinking skills by exploring a real-life situation that revolves around self-management.

Chris Dowd

Supplies and Setup: "The Procrastinators" in *On Course*

Directions:
1. [Have students read "The Procrastinators." One way to be sure everyone has read the selection before taking the next step is to have one student read the first paragraph aloud, another student read the second, and so on until the reading is complete.] [5 minutes]
2. [Find out by a show of hands how many students have picked each character as having the more challenging self-management problem. In the unlikely event that everyone chooses the same character, attempt to sway some students by playing devil's advocate. Once you have reasonable diversity of opinion, move on to Step 3.] [3–10 minutes]
3. [Create groups of like-minded students.] *Since you agree in your group about which student has the more challenging self-management problem, decide how you are going to persuade another group to agree.* [5–10 minutes]
4. [Have a spokesperson from each group present the group's position; then lead a debate on the issue by moving the discussion back and forth, allowing students to explain their positions in more detail and rebut opposing views. Where possible, elicit students' personal experiences with self-management problems. Invite students to demonstrate a change in their opinion by getting up and going to the other group.] [5–20 minutes]
5. [Create the role-play suggested in the second question of "The Procrastinators." One student role-plays Tracy or Ricardo; another student role-plays a mentor suggesting specific self-management strategies that Tracy or Ricardo could use to get on course in college.] [5–15 minutes]
6. [Lead a discussion of the "Diving Deeper" question at the end of the case study.] [5–20 minutes]
7. [Journal Writing and/or Class Discussion] *What did you learn from this discussion about self-management? What's the life lesson here?* [e.g., Feeling overwhelmed can be the result of bad self-management decisions.] [5–10 minutes]

Approximate Time: 25–55 minutes

Instructor Notes:
1. So as not to stifle discussion, I don't reveal which student I think has the most challenging self-management problem.
2. This class discussion is an excellent prewriting activity to be followed by students writing a persuasion essay that supports their opinion in the debate. Because students are now sharply aware of views opposing their own, they often write much more thorough and persuasive essays than would be the case without the debate.

Journal 14.   Believing in Yourself: Develop Self-Confidence

EXERCISE 14-1: Victories

Purpose: To offer students an opportunity to acknowledge their successes, thus building self-confidence.

Supplies and Setup: Chime; students (A & B) sitting in pairs

Directions:
1. *Everyone has accomplished goals, and each goal—whether large or small—is a personal victory. Victims focus on what they have not accomplished in life; Creators acknowledge their victories in life.* [1 minute]
2. *When I say go, start telling each other about some of your victories in life. Alternate back and forth, sharing as many victories as you can as fast as you can. After a minute, I'll ring the chime and call for either A's or B's to "FLY." That person will leap up, find an empty seat, sit down with a new partner, and immediately start exchanging victories. Again, go back and forth, telling each other about victories you have created in your life. Then I'll ring the chime and shout for A's or B's to "FLY" again, and one of you will dash off to a new partner to do it all over again.* [DEMO the process, telling your victories quickly to model a sense of urgency.] [3–5 minutes]
3. *So, any questions? Get ready, and start telling your victories NOW!* [6–10 minutes, depending on how many partner changes you want]
4. [Freewriting/Class Discussion] *What was your experience? What was it like to hear your partner telling you about victories? What was it like to speak of your own victories? Did your Inner Critic try to block you from telling your victories? How? How do you feel right now? What would it do for your self-confidence if you acknowledged your victories more often? What's the life lesson here?* [e.g., I've got more victories than I thought I did, and saying them out loud makes me feel proud of what I've accomplished.] [10–20 minutes]

Approximate Time: 20–30 minutes

Instructor Notes:
1. Some Inner Critics will accuse the students of "bragging." I acknowledge to students that they might not want to go around telling everyone about their victories, but they surely would get value from acknowledging them to close friends and to themselves.
2. You can use the same process to have students acknowledge their talents, skills, and personal strengths.

EXERCISE 14-2: Visualizing My Success

Purpose: To practice visualizing successfully doing a purposeful action.

Supplies and Setup: Groups of 5 to 6 students standing in a circle. [Equipment for optional step: Video camera and VCR/TV for playback]

Directions:
1. *Think of one of your most challenging goals. Now think of a **purposeful** action that you need to take to achieve this goal. Even better is to think of a **purposeful** action that you've been avoiding for some reason.* [After 1–2 minutes, ask:] *Has everyone thought of a **purposeful** action you could take?* [Give more time or coaching, if necessary.]
2. *Each of you will act out your **purposeful** action, and your group will try to guess what it is that you're doing. Each person will have 2 minutes.* [You might want to DEMO acting out 1 of your own purposeful actions, like sitting down to grade a set of exams or painting your living room.] [10 minutes]
3. [Optional: Videotape one or more students from each group acting our their visualization. You can then show the scenes to the whole class for discussion.]
4. [Freewriting and/or Class Discussion] *What did you learn about visualizing from this exercise? What's the life lesson here?* [*e.g.,* Visualizing myself doing something scary makes it seem less intimidating.] [5–10 minutes]

Approximate Time: 15–25 minutes

Instructor Notes:
1. Here's an alternative that requires time outside of class. Put students in pairs. Give each student the assignment to choose and actually carry out a purposeful action that will move him or her toward an important goal, especially one he or she has been postponing. Partners videotape each other doing the action (like going to see a teacher for a conference or studying for a math test). This approach, of course, requires arranging for the students to have access to a video camera, but it may be that enough students in your class have video cameras of their own. With this approach, you can show the videotapes in class, then discuss the power of actually seeing the purposeful action being done.

EXERCISE 14-3: Talents

Purpose: To offer students an opportunity to acknowledge their talents and skills.

Supplies and Setup: Entire class standing in a large circle

Directions:
1. *Creators raise their self-esteem by acknowledging their talents and skills, at least to themselves. They're good at certain things and, without being conceited, they know it. So be a Creator and think of a talent or a skill that you have. You don't need to be an expert, just think of something that you're fairly good at.* [2 minutes]
2. *When you're ready, you'll walk into the middle of the circle and tell us one thing that you're good at. Anyone else with that same talent will affirm it by also stepping into the circle. We'll applaud to acknowledge you all for your talents and skills. Then return to the outside circle, and someone else will step into the circle and tell us one of his or her talents. You can go as many times as you want; just be aware of those who haven't had a chance to go. Notice if your Inner Critic or Inner Defender tries to block you from telling us your talents.* [2 minutes for directions]

3. *So, I'll start. "I'm good at . . ."* [Tell something you're good at, invite others with the same talent or skill to step into the circle with you, and urge those in the outside circle to give resounding applause. Encourage an enthusiastic response to set the pattern for students who follow you. Then take your place in the circle and wait for others to do what you've modeled.] [5–15 minutes, depending on the size of the group and energy generated by the exercise.]

4. [Freewriting/Discussion] *What was your experience? What was it like to tell about your talents? What was it like to acknowledge that you have talents that someone else named? What was it like to be applauded for your talents? To applaud others? Did your Inner Critic or Inner Defender try to block you from telling or acknowledging your talents? What was the chatter in your head? How did you respond? How do you feel right now? What would it do for your self-confidence if you acknowledged your talents often? What's the life lesson here?* [e.g., It's a lot easier to acknowledge other people for their talents than it is to acknowledge myself for my own talents.]

Approximate Time: 20–30 minutes

Instructor Notes:

1. By this time in the semester, most students will be comfortable coming into the circle. If you have a few shy students, you might (near the end of the allotted time) say, "Some of you haven't chosen to go yet, and that's okay. But this is a great opportunity for you to experiment with a bold new behavior. What do you say? We'll give you extra applause. C'mon, you can do it!!" The key here is to be encouraging without singling anyone out. Almost always a few shy students will say, "Oh, all right . . ." and you've helped them choose an empowering new behavior.

CHAPTER 4: Quiz Questions

11. Acting on Purpose

For questions 1–4, choose two of the following to fill in the blanks:

IMPORTANT, UNIMPORTANT, URGENT, NOT URGENT

1. Quadrant I actions are _____ and _____.
2. Quadrant II actions are _____ and _____.
3. Quadrant III actions are _____ and _____.
4. Quadrant IV actions are _____ and _____.
5. Creators spend as much time as possible in Quadrant _____.

Answers: 1. IMPORTANT and URGENT 2. IMPORTANT and NOT URGENT 3. UNIMPORTANT and URGENT 4. UNIMPORTANT and NOT URGENT 5. II

12. Mastering Effective Self-Management

1. It is possible to manage time. TRUE FALSE
2–4. Three helpful tools for effective self-management are (2) _____, (3) _____, and (4) _____.
5. A(n) _____ helps you track your actions and confirm that you are doing what you planned to do.

Answers: 1. FALSE (We can only manage ourselves, our own actions.) 2. monthly calendar 3. next actions list 4. 32-day commitment *Note: Answers to questions 2–4 can be presented in any order.* 5. tracking form

13. Developing Self-Discipline

1. Self-discipline is commitment made visible through purposeful actions. TRUE FALSE
2–4. Self-discipline has three essential ingredients: (2) _____, (3) _____, and (4) _____.
5. People are either born with self-discipline or they're not. TRUE FALSE

Answers: 1. TRUE 2. commitment 3. focus 4. persistence 5. FALSE
Note: Answers to questions 2–4 can be presented in any order.

14. Believing in Yourself: Develop Self-Confidence

1. Self-esteem is strengthened by increased self-confidence. TRUE FALSE
2. Self-confidence is the core belief that I _____.
3. By creating one small success after another, eventually you create a success _____, which is one way to build your self-confidence.
4. A way to build your self-confidence is to celebrate your _____ and talents.
5. Another way to build your self-confidence is to _____ yourself doing purposeful actions successfully.

Answers: 1. TRUE 2. can 3. identity 4. successes or skills or victories 5. visualize

CHAPTER 4: Essay Topics

1. Students new to college are often overwhelmed by their newfound freedom to make almost unlimited choices. As a result of bad choices, some first-year students do much less well than they are capable of doing. Write an essay in which you warn these students about the bad choices they will probably be tempted to make and recommend the most important actions they should take to resist those temptations and be successful in college.
2. Choosing to do a 32-Day Commitment offers you an intense learning experience. Write an essay for your classmates in which you discuss your experience with your 32-Day Commitment, including the life lessons you learned from the experience. Consider, among other things, how your thoughts, feelings, and actions changed over the course of the 32 days. It is not necessary that you had a successful 32-Day Commitment to write this essay. In fact, there will be much to learn from a 32-Day Commitment that you had trouble keeping.
3. Many people find that they don't get as much accomplished in their lives as they want. Yet they resist undertaking any sort of self-management system, saying they aren't comfortable using tools like a monthly calendar, next-action list, 32-day commitment, or a tracking form. Write an essay for people who have difficulty using a written self-management plan, suggesting how they might accomplish more in their lives with self-management strategies that are consistent with their personalities. As much as possible, use your own experience to support your opinions.
4. There are numerous commercial time-management tools and systems on the market today (*e.g.*, Palm Pilot, BlackBerry, Franklin Covey Planner, Day Runner, Day Timer, etc.). Go to an office

supply store and familiarize yourself with a number of options available. Then write a consumer report essay in which you compare the strengths and weaknesses of various products. If you find one that you believe is clearly superior to the rest, make your case for it.

5. One of the ways that people build confidence is by taking positive risks. Write an essay in which you fully describe the biggest risk(s) you have taken in your life, what you learned from your experience(s), and how your overall confidence has been affected.

6. People's confidence in their ability to succeed at something has a great deal to do with the level of their eventual success. Write an essay for fellow college students in which you explain how confident you feel about succeeding in college. Fully explore what you believe are the causes of your present level of academic confidence, and propose what you will do to raise your confidence higher.

Chapter 5
Developing Interdependence

Concept

The world provides valuable resources for those who choose interdependence over independence, dependence, and codependence. Many students, however, do not utilize the abundant human resources available to assist them to more easily and enjoyably achieve their goals. Worse, many students are entangled in a web of toxic relationships. Without positive assistance, many students find the achievement of personal, academic, and professional goals to be difficult, even impossible. By offering students the skills to build and nurture mutually supportive relationships, we empower them to benefit from resources that might otherwise go untapped, to experience the uplift of giving and receiving assistance, and to achieve goals that otherwise might be difficult or even impossible.

Empowers Students to . . .

1. Develop interdependence, reinforcing mutual cooperation rather than competition.
2. Identify valuable resources that can assist them in reaching their goals.
3. Request assistance in achieving their goals.
4. Create a network of support for college and beyond.
5. Develop personal bonds of friendship and appreciation that can support them to persist in a course or in college.
6. Communicate more effectively both as a speaker and a listener.
7. Reduce anxiety and reluctance about trusting others, increasing a sense of safety and willingness to interact positively with the people in their lives.

Remember to consider using the all-purpose exercises mentioned in the introduction, especially JOURNAL READINGS, QUOTATIONS, POEMS, CARTOONS, FOCUS QUESTIONS, AND CHAPTER-OPENING SUMMARIES. Remind students to use letters to label any in-class writing they do in their journals.

Journal 15.   Developing Mutually Supportive Relationships

EXERCISE 15-1: The Chair Lift

Purpose: To demonstrate that some goals are difficult, or even impossible, to achieve alone, but they are relatively easy to accomplish with help.

Supplies and Setup: Two volunteers (ideally volunteer A should be larger than volunteer B); one chair. Have volunteer A (the larger person) sit in the chair and volunteer B stand behind the chair.

Directions:

1. *Everyone in the room will have a goal during this activity.* [To the class] *Your goal is to listen to the goal I give to B and decide how you would attempt to accomplish the goal.* [To A] *You've got the easiest goal of all. Your goal is to stay seated in the chair. You may not stand up. Can you handle that?* [To B] *Your goal is to cause the chair with A sitting in it to be eighteen inches in the air as soon as possible. That is, every part of the chair and A, including feet, must be at least a foot and a half in the air. Ready? Go.* [It's important that you say "cause the chair," not "lift the chair."] [2 minutes]

2. [Listen for B's self-talk. B's Inner Critics will very likely say things like, "I can't do that" or "I'm not strong enough." Whatever B says for now, simply repeat the directions.] *Remember, your goal is to cause the chair with A sitting in it to be eighteen inches in the air as soon as possible. That is, every part of the chair and A, including feet, must be at least a foot and a half in the air. Ready? Go.* [2–5 minutes]

3. [Now, encourage B, saying that the goal *can* be accomplished with the right approach. If B doesn't achieve the goal after a couple of minutes, ask B if the class can offer suggestions. Eventually, someone will suggest that B needs help. If B asks, "Can I ask for help?" simply repeat the directions, stressing "**cause** the chair." Notice that you have never told B to lift the chair. Eventually, you will have volunteers come to help B lift the chair with A in it. **IMPORTANT:** Be sure there are at least four strong people lifting, and ask each one if his or her back is okay. Tell them to lift with their legs, not their backs. The point here is to guard against injury. I have done this activity many times, and no one has ever gotten hurt . . . but I am always very careful!] [2–5 minutes]

4. [Freewriting and/or Class Discussion] [To B] *So, what's the life lesson of the chair-lift exercise?* [A goal that I couldn't accomplish alone became easy with help.] *Can you identify other goals you have that are difficult because you're trying to accomplish them alone? Whom could you ask for help? Will you? When is it best to be independent and when is it best to be interdependent?* [These same questions can also be asked of the rest of the students.] [2–5 minutes]

Approximate Time: 5–20 minutes

Instructor Notes:

1. If you noticed some self-talk that is clearly B's Inner Critic or Inner Defender at work, you might want to spend a few minutes discussing how those voices interfered with his or her success and how to work with that inner voice.

EXERCISE 15-2: The Scavenger Hunt

Purpose: To assist students to learn about your college's resources for student success and to demonstrate that some goals are impossible to achieve alone but are relatively easy to achieve with help.

Supplies and Setup: The Scavenger Hunt (next page)

Directions: IMPORTANT: Read Steps 1–5 of the **Directions** exactly as given:

1. *The way **you all** can win the Scavenger Hunt is by accumulating the maximum number of points available.*

2. *The way **you each** accumulate points is to fill in the correct answer in any of the three columns.*

3. *If **you** are a winner, you will win a prize.*

4. *Let's synchronize our watches. It's now* _____. *You must be back in this room by* _____ *to be a winner.* [Allow about 20 minutes for the Scavenger Hunt.]

Scavenger Hunt

Student Desire or Problem	Name of College Office or Resource	Location	Person to See
1. Need money for tuition and books.			
2. Can't decide what major to choose.			
3. Want to drop a course.			
4. Need tutoring in writing.			
5. Want to participate in clubs and activities.			
6. Need to withdraw from a course.			
7. Have a problem with a college bill.			
8. Feeling physically ill.			
9. Need information about transferring to another college.			
10. Need to exchange textbooks.			
11. Having a personal problem.			
12. Need a computer to type an essay.			
13. Want career information.			
14. Want to write for the school newspaper.			
15. Need tutoring in reading.			
16. Want services for disabled students.			
17. Want to serve on student government.			
18. Need books for a research paper.			
19. Want to transfer credits to another college.			
20. Need a part-time job.			
21. Need a parking permit.			
22. Want to play intramural sports.			
23. Need tutoring in math.			
24. Have complaint about a teacher.			

5. *The Scavenger Hunt will not start until everyone is ready. Are you ready?* [This is the time that students could form network teams so they could all be winners; chances are they will dash out of the door on their own.] *If ready, let the Scavenger Hunt begin.* [Steps 1–5: 3–5 minutes]

6. [Upon students' return, go over the resources they have discovered.] [10–15 minutes]

7. *Now let's see who won the Scavenger Hunt. Remember, I said, "The way **you all** can win the Scavenger Hunt is by accumulating the maximum number of points available." What is the maximum number of points available?* [72] *Did anyone score that many points? What is the only way you could win this game?* [The only way to win the game is by cooperating in a network. Discuss the students' assumption that they were in competition with one another and that only one person could be a winner when, in fact, the directions allow everyone to be a winner. In what other areas of their lives do they compete, even when cooperation would be more beneficial?] [10 minutes]

8. [Freewriting and/or Class Discussion] *What is the life lesson of the Scavenger Hunt?* [e.g., For some tasks, many people can accomplish with ease what one person cannot accomplish alone.] [5–10 minutes]

Approximate Time: 30–50 minutes

EXERCISE 15-3: The Interdependence Game

Purpose: To demonstrate the power of interdependence to solve problems.

Supplies and Setup: 1 volunteer up front; 1 recorder with pen and paper. You may wish to write the 3 sentence stems (Step 1 below) on the chalkboard or on an overhead transparency.

Directions:
1. [To the student volunteer] *We're going to play the Interdependence Game. This is a game in which you can get immediate help on a problem you have. You could leave here today with one of your problems solved. Here's how the game works. All you need to do is read and complete these three sentence stems: **My goal is . . . My problem is . . . The help I'd like is . . .** What specific help do you need to solve your problem? Do you need information? Advice? Assistance?* [DEMO the Interdependence Game process with a problem of your own, or you could tell a story of how the Interdependence Game helped someone in a previous class. For example, Vicki's goal was to move to Florida at the end of the semester; her problem was that she had to paint her house before she could sell it; she asked people to come to a painting party and help her paint the inside of her house. Three people showed up that day and helped her paint her house. One of the people helping that day was a man Vicki had never met; he had come along with his friend. Vicki and the man started dating, and Vicki decided not to move to Florida. So Vicki not only got a painted house, she got a new relationship as well. Moral: You never know what you'll get when you start asking for help.] [5 minutes]

2. [To the class] After A explains the situation, if you have information, advice, or assistance to offer, raise your hand, and A will call on you. You have 30 seconds to respond, and our recorder will write down your ideas. If your idea will take longer, give a brief explanation, and invite the volunteer to meet you after class for the full version. We'll try to get 10 ideas in 5 minutes. [Do as many additional volunteers as time allows, about 5–6 minutes each.]

3. [Freewriting and/or Class Discussion] *What is the life lesson of The Interdependence Game?* [e.g., To get the help you need, sometimes all you need to do is ask for it.] [5–10 minutes]

Approximate Time: About 10–35 minutes

Instructor Notes:

1. A key to success of the Interdependence Game is to keep it moving. Don't let suggestions for help last more than thirty seconds before you say, "What a great idea . . . how about meeting after class to finish explaining your idea. Now, quick, let's get another great idea. . . ."

Journal 16. Creating a Support Network

EXERCISE 16-1: Study-Team Bingo

Purpose: To have students begin to create study teams.

Supplies and Setup: Study-Team Bingo (next page)

Directions:

1. *In the empty boxes on the top row of your Study-Team Bingo sheet, put the names of the courses you are taking this semester, including this one. If you don't have enough courses to fill in all four columns, put our course at the top of more than one column. If you have more than four courses, write your four most challenging courses.* [2 minutes]
2. *Now we're going to play Study-Team Bingo. Your goal is first to find someone in our class who is taking one of your courses written at the top of any column. Next, go down that column and see if the person has any of the qualities described in the boxes by asking questions such as "Are you a part-time student? Have you attended another college? Do you exercise regularly?"* [1 minute]
3. *If the person answers "Yes," write the person's full name (first **and** last) in the box. You may use the same person in more than one box in a column if the description applies. Move on to another person, then another. The person who has the most boxes filled in when time is called is the winner.* [10 minutes]
4. *[Ring a chime or call "Stop."] Count the number of boxes you've filled in.* [Optional: Have the winner(s) come up front and read the name and information in each of their filled-in boxes, inviting the named person to stand. This assists everyone to learn who's in the class and what some of their skills and experiences are.]
5. *[Freewriting and/or Class Discussion] What's the life lesson here?* [e.g., Many people around me have the skills and talents to help me achieve my goals.] *How could you apply this lesson to be more successful in college and in life? Are you willing to do that? When?* [5–15 minutes]
6. *I hope you'll think about creating a study team with the people who are in your classes. Remember, there are four steps to creating a helpful study team: (1) Choose the team yourself. (2) Agree on team goals. (3) Agree on meeting times, dates, place. (4) Create team rules (e.g., to each meeting bring ten questions on 3" x 5" cards with answers and sources on back).*

Approximate Time: 15–30 minutes

Instructor Notes:

1. The movie *Stand and Deliver*—available at most video rental stores—dramatizes the value of belonging to a supportive study group and choosing a wise and caring mentor. You might want to show parts of the video in class to generate additional freewritings and class discussions.

EXERCISE 16-2: Your Relationship Bank Account

Purpose: To demonstrate how we make deposits and withdrawals from the relationship bank accounts we have with family, friends, and associates in our support network.

Study-Team Bingo

is part-time student	is part-time student	is part-time student	is part-time student
is full-time student	is full-time student	is full-time student	is full-time student
loves going to college	loves going to college	loves going to college	loves going to college
types 30 wpm or more	types 30 wpm or more	types 30 wpm or more	types 30 wpm or more
has child under 10	has child under 10	has child under 10	has child under 10
has scholarship aid	has scholarship aid	has scholarship aid	has scholarship aid
uses Microsoft Word	uses Microsoft Word	uses Microsoft Word	uses Microsoft Word
drives to school	drives to school	drives to school	drives to school
will get 4-year degree	will get 4-year degree	will get 4-year degree	will get 4-year degree
lives in your zip code	lives in your zip code	lives in your zip code	lives in your zip code
works full-time	works full-time	works full-time	works full-time
has work-study job	has work-study job	has work-study job	has work-study job
belongs to a study group	belongs to a study group	belongs to a study group	belongs to a study group
has same career goal as you	has same career goal as you	has same career goal as you	has same career goal as you
is good at math	is good at math	is good at math	is good at math
out of school 10+ years	out of school 10+ years	out of school 10+ years	out of school 10+ years
attended other college	attended other college	attended other college	attended other college
exercises regularly	exercises regularly	exercises regularly	exercises regularly
is grandparent	is grandparent	is grandparent	is grandparent
has 20+ college credits	has 20+ college credits	has 20+ college credits	has 20+ college credits

Supplies and Setup: Pen and paper

Directions:

1. *I want you to think about one of your best friends. Create a picture of this person in your mind. Now, on a sheet of paper write the number 100. This represents the present balance that your friend has in a relationship bank account with you.*

2. *I'll now ask you to imagine that your friend did the actions that I'm about to read to you. After you hear each one, make an appropriate deposit or withdrawal from your friendship account. For example, if your friend does something that strengthens your relationship, you might add ten or twenty points to his or her account. If your friend does something that weakens your relationship, you might subtract points from the account.*

    A. *You and your friend agree to meet for lunch at noon. Your friend shows up an hour late and offers no explanation. [After reading each situation, remind students to make a deposit or a withdrawal.]*

    B. *You mention to your friend that you're having difficulty understanding one of your college courses. Your friend says, "I passed that course last semester. I'll be glad to give you some help." Your friend comes to your house the next day and tutors you for two hours.*

    C. *Your friend introduces you to a new group of people, telling them that you are the best friend he or she has in the world.*

    D. *On Friday, you and your friend agree to meet at the library at 4:00 on Monday for a study session. On the way to the library on Monday, you see your friend talking and laughing with a group of people. Your friend never shows up at the library as promised. Later your friend apologizes, "I'm really sorry I didn't meet you. I tried to get there, but I was in a conference with my history teacher, and he just kept talking. There was nothing I could do."*

    E. *You're moving to a new place to live, and you've decided to move the furniture yourself. You mention to your friend that you've asked about ten people to come over on Saturday morning to help you move. Your friend doesn't offer to assist and doesn't show up on Saturday.*

    F. *A person you barely know tells you that some people were criticizing you, and your friend stood up for you. [5 minutes]*

3. *[Journal Writing and/or Class Discussion] What is the present balance in your friendship account with this person? What behavior caused you to make the biggest withdrawal from your friend's account? Why? What rule of yours did your friend keep or break? What behavior caused you to make the biggest deposit? Why? What rule of yours did your friend keep or break? What other behaviors would make a large withdrawal from or deposit to any relationship account in your life? What is the life lesson here? [e.g., Behaviors that greatly bother one person in a relationship may not bother another person much at all.] [10–25 minutes]*

Approximate Time: 15–30 minutes

Instructor Notes:

1. Points worth stressing: We deposit points when a friend lives by our rules, and we withdraw points when a friend defies our rules. You can use this exercise to preview the discussion of beliefs and rules in Chapter 6.

Journal 17. Strengthening Relationships with Active Listening

EXERCISE 17-1: Circle of Reflection

Purpose: To practice listening actively. To explore thoughts and feelings about asking for assistance.

Supplies and Setup: Students sitting in trios (A, B, & C)

Directions:
1. *We're going to practice listening actively. Here's how it works: A speaks a thought to B about asking for help. B reflects A's thoughts and feelings. A confirms or corrects. (If A corrects, B now reflects the correction.) When B has accurately reflected A's thought, B speaks a thought to C about asking for help. C reflects B's thoughts and feelings. B confirms or corrects. When C has accurately reflected B's thought, C speaks a thought to A about asking for help. And the process of reflecting keeps going around the circle.* [Sample DEMO below. Emphasize not changing speakers until the speaker confirms that the listener has gotten the thought and feeling—the complete message—correct.]
2. *Whoever isn't the speaker or the listener is the observer. The observer's job is to identify any talking that doesn't follow the reflecting format. Keep going around your circle until I call stop.* [8–10 minutes]
3. [Journal Writing and/or Class Discussion] *What was your experience when you were the active listener? What was your experience when you were being actively listened to? What was your experience when you were the guide observing? What did you learn about active listening? What did you learn about asking for help? What is the life lesson here?* [e.g., Some people listen without really hearing.] [10–20 minutes]

Approximate Time: 20–30 minutes

Instructor Notes:
1. Here's a sample DEMO as a model for the interactions:
   A to B: I really don't like asking for help. [States thought]
   B to A: What I heard is that you don't like to ask for help. [Reflection]
   A to B: That's right. [Confirms accuracy of B's reflection]
   B to C: Well, I don't mind asking for help. In fact, my brother would probably tell you that I ask for help all the time. Maybe I ask for too much help. [States thought]
   C to B: What I heard is that you don't mind asking for help. [Reflection]
   B to C: Right, but also, sometimes I think I ask for too much help. [Corrects C's Reflection]
   C to B: Okay, now I've got it. You don't mind asking for help, but you're wondering if you ask for too much help. [Reflection]
   B to C: That's it. [Confirms C's reflection]
   C to A: Actually, I've never thought much about asking for help.
   [The process returns to A for a reflection, and it keeps going around the circle until time is called.]
2. If you want to illustrate how poorly people listen to one another, show a videotape of a few minutes from one of the conflict-oriented TV talk shows, like the *Jerry Springer Show.*

EXERCISE 17-2: The Sounds of Silence

Purpose: To demonstrate the value of silence and careful observation while actively listening.

Supplies and Setup: Chime; students sitting in pairs facing one another, each with journal and a pen

Directions:
1. *The first part of this activity is to be done without talking. Please don't say a word until I tell you it's okay to talk again. Sit with your partner in total silence and observe each other. Don't say a word until I ring the chime* [or call "Stop"]. [2 minutes]
2. [Freewriting] *In your journal, write an answer to this question: What did you observe about your partner during the silence? Be complete. Later, you'll be sharing with your partner what you wrote.* [Many people will report not observing much, rather feeling uncomfortable and wondering how much longer the silence would last.] [4 minutes]
3. *Now sit with your partner again, and this time see what you can learn about him or her just by observing him or her in silence. Use your powers of observation and intuition. Don't say a word until I ring the chime* [or call "Stop"]. [2 minutes]
4. [Freewriting] *In your journal, write an answer to this question: What did you observe about your partner this time? Be complete.* [Many people will report more meaningful observations about their partners this time.] [3 minutes]
5. *Alternate reading your first entry to one another. Then read your second entry to one another. Then take a few minutes to have a conversation about what you observed and learned about each other.* [7 minutes]
6. [Freewriting and/or Class Discussion] *What was the experience like for you? What did you learn? How might silence contribute to a more complete communication? What can you look for in another person that tells you something about that person or what he or she is experiencing at the moment? What is the life lesson here?* [e.g., You can look at a person without really seeing him or her.] [5–15 minutes]

Approximate Time: 25–40 minutes

Case Study for Critical Thinking: Professor Rogers' Trial

Purpose: To develop critical thinking skills by exploring a real-life situation that revolves around interdependence and the ability to work well with others.

Supplies and Setup: "Professor Rogers' Trial" in *On Course*

Directions:
1. [Have students read "Professor Rogers' Trial." One way to be sure everyone has read the selection before taking the next step is to have one student read the first paragraph aloud, another student read the second, and so on until the reading is complete. Then have students put in their scores for the 4 characters.] [5 minutes]
2. [Find out by a show of hands how many students have picked each character as number 1—having the greatest responsibility for the teams' grade of D. If 2 or more characters are chosen as number 1, move on to Step 3. In the unlikely event that everyone chooses the same character as number 1 (or there is otherwise little diversity in opinion), ask how many students have picked each character as number 4—having the least responsibility for the team's grade of D.]

3. [Create groups of like-minded students.] *Since you agree in your group about which character has the greatest (or least) responsibility for the group's grade of D, decide how you are going to persuade others to agree with you.* [5–10 minutes]
4. [Have a spokesperson from each group present the group's position; then lead a debate on the issue by moving the discussion from group to group, allowing students to explain their positions in more detail and rebut opposing views. Invite students to demonstrate a change in their opinions by getting up and going to the group with which they now agree.] [5–20 minutes]
5. [Create the role-play suggested in the "Diving Deeper" section. A student volunteer role-plays one of the 4 characters in the story; another student role-plays a mentor offering specific advice on interdependence. Additionally, the mentor can suggest choices the character could have made earlier to prevent the problem that now exists and explore what is the best choice the character could make now. Finally the mentor can guide the character to discover what valuable life lesson is available from this experience.] [5–10 minutes]
6. [Journal Writing and/or Class Discussion] What is the life lesson here about interdependence and working collaboratively? [5–10 minutes]

Approximate Time: 25–55 minutes

Instructor Notes:
1. So as not to stifle discussion, I don't tell students what my scores are.
2. This class discussion is an excellent prewriting activity to be followed by students writing a persuasion essay supporting their opinions in the debate. Because students are now sharply aware of views opposed to their own, they often write much more thorough and persuasive essays than would be the case without the debate.

Journal 18.   Believing in Yourself: Be Assertive

EXERCISE 18-1: The Party

Purpose: To better understand placating, blaming, and leveling as communication styles.

Supplies and Setup: Chime (or another way to get the students' attention)

Directions:
1. *In a few moments, we're going to have a party of placators, blamers, and levelers. Everyone born in January, February, March, or April will communicate as placator. Those born in May, June July, or August, your style of communication will be blaming. If you were born in September, October, November, or December, your style of communication will be leveling. When you talk to people at this party, communicate in your assigned style. Let's review how placators, blamers, and levelers like to communicate.* [DEMO each of these 3 communication styles. Remind everyone that these are the voices of the Inner Critic (placating), Inner Defender (blaming), and Inner Guide (leveling).] [5–8 minutes]
2. *Okay, let the party begin!* [3–5 minutes]
3. [Ring the chime or call "Stop!"] *Stop where you are, close your eyes, and become aware of your breathing, thoughts, feelings, and body sensations.* [Pause] *How do you feel about yourself?* [Pause] *How do you feel about the people you have been talking to?* [Pause] *Now we're going to start the party again. But you're going to change communication styles. If you were placating, now use blaming. If you were blaming, now use leveling. If you were leveling, now use placating. Okay, let the party resume!* [5 minutes]

4. [Ring the chime or call "Stop!"] *Stop where you are, close your eyes, and again become aware of your breathing, thoughts, feelings, and body sensations.* [Pause] *How do you feel about yourself now?* [Pause] *How do you feel about the people you have been talking to?* [Pause] *In a moment, we're going to start the party again. But you're going to change communication styles one last time. If you were placating, now use blaming. If you were blaming, now use leveling. If you were leveling, now use placating. Okay, let the party resume!* [5 minutes]

5. [Ring the chime or call "Stop!"] *Stop where you are, close your eyes, and one more time become aware of your breathing, thoughts, feelings, and body sensations.* [Pause] *How do you feel about yourself now?* [Pause] *How do you feel about the people you have been talking to?* [Pause] *Okay, return to your seats.* [5 minutes]

6. [Freewriting and/or Class Discussion] *What was your experience at this party? How did you feel about yourself as you spoke as a placator? As a blamer? As a leveler? How did you feel about other people using these three styles to communicate with you? Did you have a sense that any of these communication styles is the one you use most often? What is the life lesson here?* [*e.g.,* Speaking as a placator and blamer is exhausting.] [10–20 minutes]

Approximate Time: 30–50 minutes

EXERCISE 18-2: Make a Request—Now!

Purpose: To assist students to be more assertive about making requests, especially at college.

Supplies and Setup: Pen and Paper

Directions:
1. *Write down a problem that you are having here at college. Perhaps you're having a problem with a particular course, or with a particular assignment, or with finding a book you need. . . . Okay, let's hear some of the problems you have.* [Having some students read their problems will assist others to think of one of their own. Make sure everyone has thought of a problem before moving on to Step 2.] [5 minutes]

2. *Now make a list of requests you could make to assist you to solve this problem. For example, if your problem is that you're confused in your math course, you could request an appointment with your math teacher or a tutor to get help. . . . Okay, let's hear your problem and the requests for help that you could make.* [As students read their lists of possible requests, listen for one in each list that the student could do immediately. Without telling them why, instruct each to put a star next to one request—the one you picked because the request could be made immediately.] [15 minutes]

3. [Each student should now have a request starred that he or she could make immediately.] *Get with a partner. You have five minutes to practice your request.* [5 minutes]

4. *Okay, now I want you to leave the class and go and make the request that has a star next to it. I want you back here in fifteen minutes to report on your experience, no matter what it is.* [15 minutes]

5. [Freewriting and/or Class Discussion] *What was your experience? Were you aware of your Inner Critic or Inner Defender talking to you as you went to make your request? How did you feel as you went to make the request? How did you feel after making the request (if you were able to)? What is the life lesson here?* [*e.g.,* Making a request that is important to me is a great way to take care of myself.] [15 minutes]

Approximate Time: 50 minutes

Instructor Notes:
  1. Some students may not have been able (either because of inner or outer barriers) to make their requests. Be sure to remind them that they don't have to judge themselves for not succeeding this time. You might even want to suggest that they create a plan to try it again and report their results in the next class period. This activity is another of life's learning opportunities, not a reason to beat up on themselves.

CHAPTER 5: Quiz Questions

15. Developing Mutually Supportive Relationships

Fill in the blanks with one of the following answers: DEPENDENT, CODEPENDENT, INDEPENDENT, INTERDEPENDENT.

  1. Adults who are _____ give too much of themselves to others.
  2. Adults who are _____ take too much from other people.
  3. Adults who are _____ prefer neither to give nor to take anything from others.
  4. Adults who are _____ find a healthy balance of giving and receiving and everyone benefits.
  5. Adults who are _____ are considered the most mature by psychologists.

Answers: 1. CODEPENDENT 2. DEPENDENT 3. INDEPENDENT 4. INTERDEPENDENT
5. INTERDEPENDENT

16. Creating a Support Network

  1. OPB stands for _____ _____ _____.
2–4. Certain steps must be taken to create an effective study group. Three suggestions given in our text are (2) _____, (3) _____, and (4) _____.
  5. Taking time to create a support network in college is one of the most important Quadrant _____ activities you can undertake.

Answers: 1. other people's brains or other people's brawn 2. choose only Creators 3. choose group goals 4. choose group rules 5. II   *Note: Answers 2–4 may be in a different order.*

17. Strengthening Relationships with Active Listening

1–4. Our text suggests four steps to becoming a more active listener. They are . . .
  1. _____
  2. _____
  3. _____
  4. _____
  5. Listening effectively means that you accept 50 percent of the responsibility for receiving the same message that the speaker is sending, uncontaminated by your own thoughts or feelings.
      TRUE   FALSE

Answers: 1. Listen to understand. 2. Clear your head and remain silent. 3. Reflect the other person's thoughts and feelings. 4. Ask the person to expand or clarify. 5. FALSE (100 percent responsibility)

18. Believing in Yourself: Be Assertive

1. Victims who _____ place themselves below others. They protect themselves from the sting of criticism and rejection by saying whatever they think will gain approval.
2. Victims who _____ place themselves above others. They protect themselves from wounds of disappointment and failure by making others responsible for their problems.
3. Creators who _____ (a term used by family therapist Virginia Satir) to tell the truth as they see it.
4. Which of the following problems could you probably get help with at your college if you made a request to the proper person? _____
   A. Academic problems
   B. Money problems
   C. Health problems
   D. Problems deciding on a career
   E. All of the above
5. The DAPPS Rule, which we use to remember the qualities of an effective goal, can also be used to remember the qualities of an effective request. The letters in DAPPS stand for dated, achievable, persona, positive, and _____.

Answers: 1. placate 2. blame 3. level 4. E (You may want to confirm that all of these services are, in fact, available at your college.) 5. specific

CHAPTER 5: Essay Topics

1. Many college students are very proud of being INDEPENDENT. Write an essay in which you persuade them that they would actually be better off if they were INTERDEPENDENT.
2. Becoming conscious of the truth about ourselves is essential for making changes and creating greater success. Write an essay in which you explore the type of relationships (dependent, codependent, independent, interdependent) you have with the most important people in your life. Identify any changes you wish to make in these relationships.
3. Successful students often create study groups. Write a formal letter to three to five fellow students in one of your present classes persuading them to join you in forming a study group. Be sure to explain what a study group is, why one is important, and how you see the group working for mutual success.
4. Very few people are truly active listeners. Do a personal research project to answer the question: What behaviors typically interfere with listening well? You should be able to gather a great deal of information simply by observing people while they are engaged in a conversation. Feel free to gather information in any way that seems appropriate to answer your question. Write an essay revealing your discoveries.
5. There are times in most people's lives when they said "Yes" because they were not assertive enough to say "No." Write an essay about a time when you said "Yes" when "No" would have been a wiser choice. Explain the situation, including your thoughts that led to saying "Yes." Describe the consequences of your "Yes" in terms of the price you later paid. End your essay by explaining what you have learned about the power of saying "No" and how you expect this discovery to affect your life in the future.

Chapter 6
Gaining Self-Awareness

Concept

Many students, despite their conscious intentions, make choices that sabotage their success. As a result of self-defeating patterns (behaviors, thoughts, emotions) and unconscious limiting beliefs, students with great potential often thwart the achievement of their most cherished goals and dreams. In effect, these students are their own greatest obstacle. By assisting students to become aware of their unconscious self-defeating patterns and limiting beliefs, we empower them to rewrite outdated life scripts and change their lives for the better.

Empowers Students to . . .

1. Recognize when they are off course from their goals and dreams.
2. Identify their own self-defeating patterns of thought, behavior, and emotion.
3. Identify their unconscious limiting beliefs about themselves, other people, the world.
4. Revise their outdated scripts, thereby becoming the author of their future lives.
5. Consciously take charge of the outcomes of their lives.

Remember to consider using the all-purpose exercises mentioned in the introduction, especially JOURNAL READINGS, QUOTATIONS, POEMS, CARTOONS, FOCUS QUESTIONS, AND CHAPTER-OPENING SUMMARIES. Remind students to use letters to label any in-class writing they do in their journals.

Journal 19. Recognizing When You Are Off Course

EXERCISE 19-1: On Course—Off Course

Purpose: To become conscious of whether one is on course or off course to one's dreams.

Supplies and Setup: Students in pairs (A & B)

Directions:
1. *Make a list of all of your life roles. Refer to Journal #7 to remind yourself of the life roles you've chosen. [3 minutes]*
2. *On a scale of 0–10, rate how "on course" you are toward your goals and dreams in each of your life roles. A score of 0 means that you are totally off course in this role. A score of 10 means that you are totally on course in this role. Scores in between indicate various degrees of being on course or off course. Listen to the information available to you from your Inner Guide and score yourself now. [3 minutes]*
3. *Partner A, tell Partner B each of your life roles and the scores you have given them. Explain each score. You have five minutes. B, use your best active listening skills. [5 minutes]*

4. *Now switch roles. Partner B, you explain your scores to Partner A, who will use his or her best listening skills. You have five minutes.* [5 minutes]
5. [Journal Writing and/or Class Discussion] *What did you discover? In what roles are you on course? In what roles are you off course? What self-sabotaging habits may have gotten you off course? What could you do about these habits? What is the life lesson here?* [e.g., If I don't pay close attention, I can be way off course and my Inner Defender won't even let me know it.] [5–15 minutes]

Approximate Time: 20–30 minutes

EXERCISE 19-2: The Air Traffic Controller

Purpose: To demonstrate the value of responding as a Creator when receiving feedback about being off course.

Supplies and Setup: Have a volunteer stand on the opposite side of the room from you.

Directions:
1. [To the volunteer] *Let's imagine for this demonstration that I'm an airplane pilot, and I am trying to fly to your airport in a terrible storm. You're the air traffic controller, and it's your job to guide me safely to your airport. If I'm headed toward you, say, "On course, on course, on course . . ." If I'm not headed toward you, say, "Off course, off course, off course . . ." Now I'm going to close my eyes because there's a storm in my life, and I can't see very well.* [Head toward the volunteer and make sure he continually says "On course, on course . . ." Now head away from the volunteer and make sure he says, "Off course, off course . . ." Once you have him trained as an air traffic controller, you can go into your DEMO of what people often do when they receive feedback that they're off course.]
2. *Notice that I'm now getting feedback saying I'm off course. How do people often act when they're told they're off course?* [Elicit and dramatize various responses: anger, blame, tears, complaints, criticism of oneself, excuses, or just sitting down and giving up.] *Are any of these responses helping me get back on course?* [Naturally, the answer is NO.]
3. *Life constantly gives us feedback when we are off course. What kind of feedback might we get that we're off course in college?* [An F on a test] *On a job?* [Demoted or fired] *Concerning our health?* [We get sick or have a heart attack.] *In a relationship?* [Someone we love decides to leave us.] *Many people, when they get feedback that they're off course, resist the feedback. Does it help us get back on course to blame, complain, make excuses, or quit? Whose voices are these, anyway?* [It's the Victim speaking from his Inner Defender and Inner Critic.]
4. *What would be a more effective way to respond to feedback that tells us we're off course?* [As a Creator listening to her Inner Guide.] *Would someone like to demonstrate how a Creator, listening to her Inner Guide, would respond to the feedback from the air traffic controller?* [Have someone take your place. Have her close her eyes and role-play the plane moving on course and off course as it makes its way toward its destination. Ideally the student will simply take the off-course feedback and use it to change direction to get back on course.]
5. [Journal Writing and/or Class Discussion] *What's the life lesson here? How do you most often respond to feedback that you're off course? Are there any changes you wish to make?* [5–10 minutes]

Approximate Time: 10–20 minutes

Journal 20.   Identifying Your Scripts

EXERCISE 20-1: What's Your Pattern?

Purpose: To dramatize and raise students' awareness about self-defeating patterns.

Supplies and Setup: Groups of 3. Character Cards (next page) cut into 8 slips of paper, each with one situation on it. Use the skit subjects suggested on the next page, or create your own.

Directions:

1. [Have someone from each group pick a Character Card with the cast and situation for the skit.] *Each group has five minutes to assign each person in the group to one of the roles in the skit. Your skit should be _____ minutes long. [See Instructor Note #1 about length of skits.] The character listed first on the Character Card will always say the first line of the skit, and the other two characters will simply play off that character's lead.*

2. *Whatever your role is, your character is to demonstrate a self-defeating pattern. You can choose one from the list of EXAMPLES OF SELF-DEFEATING PATTERNS in the text preceding Journal Entry #20, or you can simply role-play one of your own self-defeating patterns. Before each skit, character #1 will read the Character Card to the audience so we know what role each person is playing. After each skit, we'll try to guess what each character's self-defeating pattern was.* [You may wish to check with each group to see that they are, indeed, choosing self-defeating patterns to dramatize.] [5–8 minutes]

3. [Get the actors in each skit to the front of the room, and turn them loose to role-play. Remind them to read their Character Cards aloud to the audience. Time the skits, and stop them if they exceed your allotted time. After each skit, have the audience guess what self-defeating patterns each person was dramatizing.]

4. [Journal Writing and/or Class Discussion] *What did you learn about self-defeating patterns? Did you recognize yourself in any of the skits? Did you discover any patterns of thought, behavior, or emotions that you want to change? What's the life lesson here?* [10–25 minutes]

Approximate Time: 10–60 minutes, depending on how many groups and skit length.

Instructor Notes:

1. Determine the length of each skit by the amount of time you have available. If you have thirty minutes available for skits and six groups, then allot five minutes per group. That would allow about three minutes for acting out the skit and two minutes for guessing the self-defeating pattern. With any luck, the point about the self-defeating patterns will be made long before ten minutes pass.

2. To create Character Cards for class, simply duplicate the next page and cut it into eighths. If you need more than eight Character Cards, make two copies of the page and create sixteen cards. It is interesting to have two groups do the same skit to see the differences.

3. You could give out Character Cards in one class period and do the skits in the next meeting. You could also carry some skits over to another day if your students get really involved.

4. Once students are familiar with this activity, you could have each team create its own Character Cards.

Character Cards

1. **STUDENT A:** Has just gotten word that he/she has been turned down for a scholarship.
2. **DIRECTOR OF FINANCIAL AID:** This is the person who turned down Student A's application for a scholarship.
3. **STUDENT B:** The boyfriend or girlfriend of Student A. Just got a huge scholarship from the same director of financial aid.

---

1. **FRIEND #1:** Promised two friends to buy them lottery tickets for Christmas. Asked them to each pick a number, bought the tickets, and held on to them. The ticket bought for Friend #2 wins $1,000,000. Friend #1's spouse threatens a divorce if Friend #1 gives the winning ticket to Friend #2.
2. **FRIEND #2**
3. **FRIEND #3**

---

1. **THE BOSS:** Owns a huge business, is looking for a vice-president, and has narrowed the field to Applicants A & B. The Boss has invited both applicants in at the same time for a final interview.
2. **APPLICANT A**
3. **APPLICANT B**

---

1. **STUDENT #1:** Organized these three students into a study group for a very difficult course. Always comes to the group prepared.
2. **STUDENT #2:** Sometimes comes to the group prepared.
3. **STUDENT #3:** Never comes to the group prepared and often misses the meetings.

---

1. **MOTHER:** Has discovered that her teenager has not been attending high school for the last three weeks. She has no idea where her teenager has been going every day.
2. **FATHER:** Dropped out of high school when he was a teenager.
3. **TEENAGER**

---

1. **SPOUSE #1:** Wants to return to college. Has been out of school for 10 years. Presently earns more money than Spouse #2 but dislikes the job.
2. **SPOUSE #2:** Worried about their family having enough money if Spouse #1 goes to college.
3. **PARENT OF SPOUSE #2:** Visiting from another state.

---

1. **DRIVER #1:** Was backing out of a parking space in a mall parking lot and was struck in the rear door by Driver #2 who was also backing out of a parking space. Driver #1's car has a huge dent. Driver #2's car is unhurt.
2. **DRIVER #2:** Thinks that Driver #1 is at fault for backing out so fast.
3. **POLICE OFFICER**

---

1. **STUDENT:** Has failed the Professor's class; believes that the Professor graded unfairly after the Student disagreed with the Professor in front of the class; has appealed the grade to the Department Chairperson.
2. **PROFESSOR**
3. **DEPARTMENT CHAIRPERSON**

EXERCISE 20-2: The Puzzle

Purpose: To discover self-defeating patterns and their underlying limiting beliefs.

Supplies and Setup: Groups of 8 to 10 students. Each group has a jigsaw puzzle of about 35 pieces.

Directions:
1. *Your goal is to assemble the puzzles as quickly as possible. Ready, go.* [Record what people are doing/saying as they work on the puzzles.] [5–10 minutes]
2. [When all puzzles are assembled, introduce the next part as follows.] *Some psychologists believe that the microcosm of our lives (the little things) reveal the macrocosm of our lives (the big things). For example, the way you go to the grocery store may reveal how you live your life. Do you go up and down every aisle or go right to what you need? Do you buy whatever brand you want or only the ones on sale? Do you chat in the check-out line or are you all business about finishing your shopping? For today, you're going to see what you can learn about how you live your life by examining how you did the puzzle. It's important to realize that none of this exploration is about "Right" and "Wrong." It's merely about becoming aware of how we live our lives.* [Give examples of what you saw, heard, and recorded as the puzzles were being assembled.] [5 minutes]
3. *Now we're going to begin a little experiment in self-awareness. Title a page in your journal: "How I did the puzzle is how I do my life." Then write as much as you can to prove that this statement is true. Don't worry about whether it really IS true; for now, just pretend it is, and make your case by giving examples wherever possible. Consider questions such as "What were you thinking, feeling, and doing while your group was working on the puzzle? What beliefs about yourself, other people, or the world would cause you to think, feel, and do what you did?" You'll have 5–8 minutes to write; then you'll share what you wrote with someone else. By the way, everybody "did the puzzle." Whatever you did from the time I put the puzzles out until the puzzles were put together (even if you were out of the room) is "how you did the puzzle." And, once more, please understand that this is not about whether you did this activity "Right" or "Wrong." This is only about seeing how aware you are about what you were doing during the puzzle...and how often you do the same thing in other parts of your life. So go ahead and make a case for the idea, "How I did the puzzle is how I do my life."* [5–10 minutes]
4. *Now meet with a partner, and read and discuss what you wrote. See if your partner found any truth to the idea that "How I did the puzzle is how I do my life."* [10 minutes]
5. [Class Discussion] *So, did anyone find truth in the statement that "How I did the puzzle is how I do my life"? Do these habit patterns support or limit you in achieving your desired outcomes and experiences? Are there any changes you'd like to make in your beliefs, behaviors, thoughts, or feelings? What is the life lesson here?* [e.g., Self-aware people make choices with minimal contamination from their past experiences.] [10–20 minutes]

Approximate Time: 35–60 minutes

Instructor Notes:
1. This puzzle exercise is a very powerful means for generating discussion and insight about habit patterns and their underlying beliefs. Given time, many people will make extraordinary discoveries about their scripts.
2. Keep the groups large enough so that it is difficult for everyone to work on the puzzle at the same time. This arrangement creates some tension and tends to cause scripts to emerge. Among other discoveries, participants may notice their patterns of participating/withdrawing and of competing/cooperating.

Journal 21. Rewriting Your Outdated Scripts

EXERCISE 21-1: What I Did Instead

Purpose: To raise students' awareness about limiting core beliefs that may cause them to make unwise choices and how they can revise these beliefs.

Supplies and Setup: Each student needs a pen and a piece of paper.

Directions:
1. *Think of a time when you missed or were late to a class for a poor reason. On a piece of paper, write what you did instead of attending or getting to class on time. Don't put your name on the paper. For example, you might write, "Instead of going to math class, I stayed home to watch television." Or, "I stopped in the cafeteria, got into a conversation with a friend, and arrived late to English class." [3 minutes]*
2. *[Collect the papers and redistribute them so no one knows whose paper he or she has.] [2 minutes]*
3. *Look at what the person chose to do instead of attending class or being on time. Write a list of possible **limiting core beliefs** that may have led to this choice. In other words, why do you think the student REALLY was late or absent? For example, if the student chose, instead of going to English class on time, to continue a conversation with a friend in the cafeteria, you might suggest the following possible core beliefs:*

   "I'm not smart enough to pass this class."
   "Going to college is a waste of time."
   "Teachers don't care whether I do well in college."
   "When I'm tired, I'm not motivated to go to class."
   "It doesn't matter if I'm late."
   "I can't be rude and just walk away from a conversation."

4. *Now get a partner. Partner A, read the core beliefs on your list to your partner. After reading each belief, tell B whether this core belief is actually one of your own. Partner B, ask questions to help A explore each core belief and take ownership if appropriate. Discuss what would be a more empowering core belief to adopt. When I ring the chime, reverse roles. [10–15 minutes]*
5. *[Freewriting and/or Class Discussion] What did you learn about your limiting core beliefs from this activity? Did you discover a limiting core belief that you will actively seek to rewrite? What's the life lesson here? [e.g., Core beliefs that I'm not even aware of can cause me to make unwise choices. I need to become more aware of my core beliefs.] [5–15 minutes]*

Approximate Time: 25–35 minutes

Instructor Notes:
1. When students are speculating in Step 3 about the other person's limiting core beliefs, they are very likely projecting their own scripts onto another. So it is likely that at least some, if not all, of the core beliefs in their lists are actually their own.

EXERCISE 21-2: Author, Author

Purpose: To practice changing a limiting script into an empowering script.

Supplies and Setup: 10 3" x 5" cards for each student

Directions:
1. *By now you're probably aware of some of your limiting beliefs. As you know, if you revise your limiting beliefs, you'll change your patterns of thought, behavior, and emotion.*
2. *Write five limiting beliefs, one each on five 3" x 5" cards. Write limiting beliefs you have about life, about people, and especially about yourself. You can refer to the list of limiting beliefs in Section 20 of* On Course. *For example, one of the students mentioned in* On Course *believed, "I am the half-brain in the family, so I'll never be able to go to college." [5–8 minutes]*
3. *Next, translate each of your limiting beliefs into empowering beliefs. Write each empowering belief on a separate 3" x 5" card. For example, the student in* On Course *might have revised her limiting belief to read, "I am smart and doing great in college." [5–10 minutes]*
4. *Who would like to read one [or more] of your empowering scripts to the class? [5 minutes]*
5. *[Journal Writing and/or Class Discussion] When are times that it might be particularly important to remind yourself of these new beliefs? How can you remember to think these empowering beliefs even at the most difficult times? So, what's the life lesson here? [e.g., It isn't easy, but I can change my core beliefs.] [10–20 minutes]*

Approximate Time: 20–40 minutes

Instructor Notes:
1. Suggest that students carry their empowering script cards with them or post them at home where they will see them often. You can also suggest that students rip up and throw away their limiting script cards.

EXERCISE 21-3: The Paper Pull

Purpose: To discover outdated scripts.

Supplies and Setup: Students sitting in pairs facing one another. Each pair has an 8½" x 11" piece of paper.

Directions:
1. *Each of you take hold of two corners of the paper with your thumbs and forefingers. Imagine that this piece of paper represents one of your greatest dreams. Perhaps your dream is a great job, a college degree, perfect health, a happy family . . . whatever you dream of having, doing, or being. That means the paper may represent different things to each of you. When I say "Go," you'll have two minutes to get sole possession of the piece of paper. You see, in this game, only the person who gets the paper will experience his or her dream. The other person will never get his or her dream, and you can't share your dream with your partner. You can use any method you want to get sole possession of the piece of paper. But if the paper is damaged or torn in any way, neither of you will achieve your dream. Any questions? Ready? Start. [2 minutes]*
2. *[Journal Writing and/or Class Discussion] So, what happened in your pair? Did you get the paper or not? What did you **do** during the paper pull? What did you **think**? What did you **feel**? Do you see anywhere else in your life where you reach as you did in the paper pull? Do these actions, thoughts, or feelings support or limit you in achieving your goals and dreams? Are there any changes you want to make in your patterns of actions, thoughts, or emotions? What's the life lesson here? [e.g., When I feel stressed, I go for the outcome I want and give little thought to how my actions may be affecting other people.] [10–50 minutes]*

Approximate Time: 25–55 minutes

Source: This exercise is a variation of an idea by John Bradshaw.

Instructor Notes:
1. Don't push participants to identify their self-defeating patterns and limiting beliefs. Just ask the questions and let the answers come of their own accord. Expect resistance. Days or weeks later some participants will acknowledge patterns that became apparent in this simple activity.

Case Study for Critical Thinking: Strange Choices

Purpose: To develop critical thinking skills by exploring a real-life situation that revolves around self-awareness and the power of scripts to affect our choices.

Supplies and Setup: "Strange Choices" in *On Course*

Directions:
1. [Have students read "Strange Choices." One way to be sure everyone has read the selection before taking the next step is to have one student read the first paragraph aloud, another student read the second, and so on until the reading is complete. Then have students put in their scores for the six characters.] [5 minutes]
2. [Find out by a show of hands how many students have picked each Professor's student as number 1—demonstrating the most self-sabotaging script. If 2 or more characters are chosen as number 1, move on to Step 3. In the unlikely event that everyone chooses the same character as number 1 (or there is otherwise little diversity in opinion), ask how many students have picked each character as number 6—demonstrating the least self-sabotaging script. Sometimes there is more diversity in opinion here.] [3 minutes]
3. [Create groups of like-minded students.] *Since you agree in your group about which student demonstrated the most (or least) self-sabotaging script, decide how you are going to persuade other groups to agree with you.* [5–10 minutes]
4. [Have a spokesperson from each group present the group's position; then lead a debate on the issue by moving the discussion from group to group, allowing students to explain their positions in more detail and rebut opposing views. Invite students to demonstrate a change in their opinions by getting up and going to the group with which they now agree.] [5–20 minutes]
5. [Lead a discussion of the "Diving Deeper" question at the end of the case study.] [5–20 minutes]
6. [Journal Writing and/or Class Discussion] *What did you learn from this discussion about scripts, self-awareness, and the importance of conscious choices? What's the life lesson here?* [e.g., When people do something totally unexpected or self-sabotaging, there's a good chance that their script has taken control of their choice-making process.] [5–10 minutes]

Approximate Time: 25–55 minutes

Instructor Notes:
1. So as not to stifle discussion, I don't tell students what my scores are.
2. This class discussion is an excellent prewriting activity to be followed by students writing a persuasion essay supporting their opinions in the debate. Because students are now sharply aware of opposing views to their own, they often write much more thorough and persuasive essays than would be the case without the debate.

Journal 22. Believing in Yourself: Write Your Own Rules

EXERCISE 22-1: Changing Habits

Purpose: To see that rules followed over time become habits; to identify and modify self-defeating habits and rules.

Supplies and Setup: Students sitting in pairs (A & B). Write the following 3 sentence stems on the chalkboard (or put on overhead transparency):
1. **One habit I have that supports my success is . . .**
2. **One habit I have that hinders my success is . . .**
3. **One habit I would benefit from having is . . .**

Directions:
1. *Partner A will read and complete the three sentences until I call "Stop." For example, you might say . . .*
   1. *One habit I have that supports my success is . . . I always get places on time.*
   2. *One habit I have that hinders my success is . . . my smoking.*
   3. *One habit I would benefit from having is . . . exercising more.*
   Remember that habits include behaviors, thoughts, feelings, and beliefs. Keep going until I call stop.
2. *Partner B, tell Partner A what you heard him or her say. For example, "I heard you say that your smoking is a habit that hinders your success. And I heard you say that you always get places on time." [3–5 minutes]*
3. *[Reverse roles and repeat Steps 1 and 2.] [3–5 minutes]*
4. *[Freewriting and/or Class Discussion] What are some of the habits you mentioned that support your success? That hinder your success? Are there any habits that you would like to get rid of? Are there any new habits that you would like to adopt? How could you do that? How are habits like rules? What is the life lesson here? [e.g., I need to make a habit of not letting habits run my life.] [10–15 minutes]*

Approximate Time: 15–30 minutes

Instructor Notes:
1. An important point to bring out in the discussion is that the rules we adopt—whether consciously or unconsciously—eventually turn into habits. It isn't easy to adopt a new habit or eliminate an old habit, but we can choose to do that. You may wish to conclude this activity by inviting students to make a 32-Day Commitment (Journal Entry #13) to create an empowering new habit or extinguish a self-sabotaging old one.

EXERCISE 22-2: Role Model Rules

Purpose: To discover a mentor who models excellence in the way he or she lives and to determine the habits or rules the mentor uses to create success.

Supplies and Setup: Students in groups of 3 with journals

Directions:
1. *Write the name of a person who, in your opinion, has created success as you define it. This role model can be anyone, whether you know the person or not. [1–2 minutes]*

2. *Under your role model's name, list all of the reasons why you chose this person. In other words, what has this person accomplished, and what does this person do consistently that impresses you?* [5 minutes]

3. *Given what your role model has accomplished and what this person does consistently, what are most likely his or her habits or rules for life? Make a list. For example, your role model's rules might include: "Do all tasks with excellence. Perform good deeds for others. Be cheerful."*

4. *Now, each person in your group will read aloud what he or she wrote, both why you chose your role model and what his or her rules may be. Choose one person to start and go clockwise until everyone has had a chance to read.* [10 minutes]

5. [Freewriting and/or Class Discussion] *What's on your mind right now? What did you learn about creating greater success in your life? Is there one new success rule you would benefit from adopting today? What's the life lesson here?* [e.g., People don't get to be successful by accident; they operate by personal rules that act as an inner compass, and this compass keeps them on course.] [5–15 minutes]

Approximate Time: 25–40 minutes

CHAPTER 6: Quiz Questions

19. Recognizing When You Are Off Course

1. Leverrier predicted that an invisible planet was pulling the planet Uranus off its predicted course around the sun. Likewise, human beings are pulled off course by the invisible forces of their _____.
    A. conscious minds
    B. unconscious minds
    C. Inner Guide
2. Many people participate in self-sabotage by choosing actions, thoughts, and/or emotions that get them off course from their goals and dreams. TRUE FALSE
3. When Creators are off course, they tend to deny it, make excuses, blame others, or give up. TRUE FALSE
4. One characteristic of Creators is that they are able to recognize and acknowledge when they are off course. TRUE FALSE
5. The story of Jerome, the accounting student, illustrates that once a person has a clear goal he will not get off course. TRUE FALSE

Answers: 1. B 2. TRUE 3. FALSE 4. TRUE 5. FALSE

20. Identifying Your Scripts

1. Eric Berne, the creator of a mode of counseling called Transactional Analysis, referred to our invisible inner forces as _____.
2. Each of us has developed three kinds of habit patterns: actions, thoughts, and emotions. TRUE FALSE
3. Our habit patterns are motivated by our unconscious core _____.

4. We seem to create our scripts as a result of _____.
    A. how others respond to us
    B. the attributions and injunctions that significant adults tell us
    C. our observations of the behaviors of significant adults in our lives
    D. our responses to physical, mental, and emotional wounds
    E. all of the above
5. The purpose of our scripts is to maximize our pleasure and minimize our _____.

Answers: 1. scripts 2. TRUE 3. beliefs 4. E 5. pain

21. Rewriting Your Outdated Scripts

1. Diana, the student in a writing course, had a script from her childhood that said her brain didn't work well. TRUE FALSE
2. When our core beliefs about ourselves, about other people, or about the world are inaccurate, they can sabotage our success. TRUE FALSE
3. Diana's core beliefs about her ability to think caused her to hear what she expected to hear rather than what her teacher actually said. TRUE FALSE
4. Human beings can revise their limiting beliefs and change their self-defeating habit patterns. TRUE FALSE
5. The parts of our scripts that are available to our conscious minds are our patterns of self-defeating actions, thoughts, and emotions. It is by revising these three parts that we ultimately revise our limiting _____.

Answers: 1. TRUE 2. TRUE 3. TRUE 4. TRUE 5. core beliefs

22. Believing in Yourself: Write Your Own Rules

1. According to psychologist Virginia Stir, we are all living by rules, though we may not be aware of them. TRUE FALSE
2–4. According to the author of *On Course*, college instructors that he polled consistently identify three behaviors that their most successful students demonstrate. These students: _____, _____ and _____.
5. A personal rule is your conscious intention. You may need to break one of your rules if something of a higher _____ conflicts with it.

Answers: 1. TRUE 2–4. Show up, Do their best work, Participate actively. (These three answers may be in any order, and appropriate variations should be accepted, such as "attend" for "show up.") 5. value

CHAPTER 6: Essay Topics

1. One of the most important qualities of successful people is their ability to identify the life roles in which they are off course. Write an essay in which you identify the life role in which you are the most off course. Discuss what you believe is the underlying cause (self-defeating patterns and limiting core beliefs) of your being off course in this role, and present a detailed plan of action for getting back on course. Let your plan contain both outer steps (changes in actions) and inner steps (changes in beliefs and attitudes).

2. We human beings are creatures of habit. Some of our habits (or patterns) support our success, while others get us off course from our goals and dreams. Write an essay in which you thoroughly explore one of your limiting patterns of actions, thoughts, or feelings. Then discuss how you may have come to adopt this pattern, and explain how this pattern hinders you in the pursuit of a rich, personally fulfilling life. Finally, discuss a plan for changing this pattern so that you can stay on course to your goals and dreams.

3. We adopted many of our present beliefs during our childhoods. We learned these beliefs from our parents and other significant adults. These beliefs—some empowering us, some limiting us—often remain unconscious and control what we do, think, and feel. Identify one or more of your limiting beliefs, discuss how you may have come to believe it, and explain how it has limited you in the past. Finally, explain what you plan to do to revise this belief so that you can change the outcome of your future.

4. Too many people set goals for themselves that are below what they are capable of achieving. Examine your present goals and consider if you have undershot your true potential. If you now believe that you have chosen goals that are too modest, write an essay in which you explore your belief system to uncover the limiting core beliefs that are holding you back. Explore where these beliefs may have come from, and suggest what you plan to do to raise your goals in line with your true abilities.

5. Olympic gold medalist Jesse Owens said, "The battles that count aren't the ones for gold medals. The struggles within yourself—the invisible, inevitable battles inside all of us—that's where it's at." In an essay to be read by your classmates in this course, explore your own inner struggles. What inner forces have you done battle with, what has the battle been about, which side is presently winning, and what do you plan to do to triumph?

6. Children learn many of their inner rules from parents or other significant adults. Write a formal essay that you will present to an important child on his or her twenty-first birthday. In this essay, inform him or her of the most important rules you have chosen to guide your actions in life and propel you toward a rich, personally fulfilling life.

Chapter 7
Adopting Lifelong Learning

Concept

Many adults have difficulty learning because they lack beliefs, attitudes, and behaviors (scripts) that maximize learning. *To learn* means to change, and for many, moving out of their comfort zone generates anxiety and fear. Many students have academic difficulties because they perceive school as a source of boredom (too little challenge) or danger (too much challenge). These students have abandoned the insatiable curiosity and effective learning strategies that served them so effectively as young children. Exciting forays into the mysteries of the unknown have been replaced by self-preserving strategies of compliance or defiance. By familiarizing struggling students with the habitual beliefs, attitudes, and behaviors of effective learners, we offer them the opportunity to replace their ineffective choices with more effective choices that can enable them to reach their potential. In other words, in addition to teaching skills and facts, we need to help students learn why they don't learn as well as they could and how they can improve their own learning. We need to help students learn about the learner—how they presently hinder their learning and how they can make changes to maximize their learning. If we move from the present model of additive education to a model of transformational education, we will help students (re)discover the most valuable learning tool they will need for the twenty-first century: their innate human wisdom.

Empowers Students to . . .

1. Regain their natural curiosity and love of learning.
2. Rediscover an effective process for learning any new skill, fact, or concept.
3. Discover their preferred learning style.
4. Adopt the beliefs and attitudes of effective learners, replacing fear of failure with a learning orientation to life, a sense that life is a school and the only failure is to quit learning.
5. Use feedback from all sources—including mistakes, failures, obstacles, and adversities—to correct course and stay on course to their goals and dreams, learning true wisdom as they do.
6. Learn what they need to know to accomplish their greatest goals and dreams.

Remember to consider using the all-purpose exercises mentioned in the introduction, especially JOURNAL READINGS, QUOTATIONS, POEMS, CARTOONS, FOCUS QUESTIONS, AND CHAPTER-OPENING SUMMARIES. Remind students to use letters to label any in-class writing they do in their journals.

Journal 23. Discovering Your Preferred Learning Style

EXERCISE 23-1: The Learning Game

Purpose: To identify the essential steps of the learning process.

Supplies and Setup: A dollar bill folded to a very small square; one volunteer (A)

Directions:

1. *Do you remember how you loved to learn as a child and how good you were at it? Many adults have lost both this love of learning and the effective way they went about learning as a child. Today we're going to play a game to see if we can rediscover some of that lost love and the natural learning process we can use even today to maximize our learning.* [To Volunteer A] *I'm going to ask you to go out of the room for a few minutes while we set up a learning game for you to play.*

2. [To the class after A has left the room] *I'd like someone to hide this dollar bill somewhere in the room. It's important that everyone knows where the dollar is, so watch carefully where it's being hidden. When A returns, I'll tell her that her goal is to learn where the dollar is hidden. Notice how this situation is similar to coming into a new course. Your job as a student is to figure out where the valuable information—whether it's history, English, math, whatever—is hidden. In this activity, your job is to be scientists and figure out what the steps are for effective learning. Also watch for choices that defeat learning. To do that, watch and listen for everything that A does or says. See what she does that works to learn where the dollar is and what she does that doesn't work.*

   There are two parts to this activity. First, we'll just let A look for the dollar without any help. If she asks you a question, don't answer in any way. Second, after a couple of minutes, I'll fold my arms across my chest like this. That will be your signal to start giving A some feedback. Do you remember the kids' game called "Hot and Cold"? Well, as A gets closer to the dollar bill, we'll all start to hum like this: Hmmmmmmmmm. If she gets closer to the dollar, we'll hum louder. If A stops or turns away from the dollar, we'll immediately stop humming. Watch very carefully what A does both before and after we give her feedback by humming. Write down everything she says or does. Remember, you're trying to figure out what behaviors help people learn something. [5 minutes]

3. [To A after returning to the room] *We've hidden a dollar bill somewhere in this room. Your goal is to learn where it is as fast as possible. Please verbalize what you are thinking so we can understand how you learn where the dollar is. When you find the dollar, it's yours to keep. Any questions?* [No matter what the volunteer says, merely repeat these 4 sentences of direction. After a while, the volunteer will get the point and probably start looking.] [2 minutes]

4. [As the volunteer is looking for the dollar, you want to do 2 things: (1) Ask the volunteer to think out loud—explain what she is doing to try to learn where the dollar is. (2) Keep comparing what the volunteer is doing to what happens to many students in college. For example, if the volunteer gets frustrated because she is getting no answers to her questions, ask, "Have you ever had a teacher who didn't seem to give you helpful feedback? What did you do?" If the volunteer just stands and does nothing, ask, "Have you ever gotten stuck in a course and found it hard to do anything? Did doing *nothing* ever help you learn? What did?" If the volunteer says, "I quit. I just can't find it," ask, "Have you ever felt like quitting a difficult course?" The possibilities of the volunteer's actions are many, so to facilitate this activity well, you need to stay alert.] [3–8 minutes. Cut the activity shorter if the volunteer is getting too frustrated. Most volunteers will go as long as you wish, so you can gauge the duration on how long you think the class is getting value from observing the activity.]

5. [After a couple of minutes of A's searching, fold your arms to let the class know it's time for them to give feedback to the volunteer by humming. Keep asking the volunteer to think out loud: "How are you now going about trying to learn where the dollar is?" Also keep relating the

present events to the students' experiences in college: "Is it possible that you had a teacher who was giving you great feedback about how to learn a subject, but you just didn't realize what he was doing?"] [3–8 minutes, again gauging the timing on the value present]

6. [After the volunteer has found the dollar and the class has given a huge round of applause—which is usually spontaneous in this activity—then comes Journal Writing and/or Class Discussion.] *What did you learn about learning? What actions help people learn?* [There are many "right" answers here, but a few you may want to highlight are (1) ask Creator questions, (2) gather relevant information, (3) discover empowering answers, (4) test your present answers, (5) heed feedback, and (6) revise your answers when incorrect.] *What actions hinder learning? What thoughts help people learn? What thoughts hinder learning? What emotions help people learn? What emotions hinder learning? What beliefs help people learn? What beliefs hinder learning? Are there any changes you want to make to become a better learner? What is the life lesson here?* [e.g., Learning is a skill, and I can learn to learn better than I do now.] [10–25 minutes]

Approximate Time: 25–60 minutes

Instructor Notes:
1. Don't let the lengthy directions scare you. This is one of my favorite classroom activities. Students love it, and it never fails to generate fascinating discoveries about learning and about life. The Learning Game has turned out somewhat differently every time I've done it. I find this unpredictability to be part of the magic of this activity. You just need to keep your goal (discovering how people learn) in mind and go with the flow. Let the learning be yours, too.
2. The directions here are very important. It is essential that the class members understand that they are to hum as the volunteer moves *toward* the dollar and to stay quiet when the volunteer *stops or moves away* from the dollar. If, during the game, it becomes apparent that the class is sending confusing feedback to the volunteer, ask the volunteer to leave the room again, and clarify the directions for the class.
3. The volunteer will likely get frustrated after a few minutes. That's usually okay, but be sensitive not to let the frustration go on too long. Keep giving the volunteer praise and support. Don't let the volunteer stop without the experience of success in finding the dollar bill—even if you have to virtually lead him or her to it (which isn't likely).

EXERCISE 23-2: Beautiful Questions

Purpose: To offer practice in asking beautiful Creator questions, rekindling curiosity and wonderment. To have students define the important questions for courses they are taking.

Supplies and Setup: Journals; five 3" x 5" cards for each student. Students in groups of 4

Directions:
1. *The poet e.e. cummings wrote, "Always the beautiful answer / Who asks a more beautiful question." Open your journal to a clean page, and title the page "BEAUTIFUL QUESTIONS." Now make a list of some of the beautiful questions that you'd like to find answers to during your life. You have ten minutes to make your list of questions. To help yourself invent questions, think of your life roles. What do you want to know about being a student, a parent, a spouse, an employee, an athlete? Think of questions you'll need answers to in order to reach your goals and dreams.* [10 minutes] [If time allows, have students share some of their questions with the class.]

2. *Perhaps you never realized that what makes one college course different from another is their intention to answer different questions. A psychology course, for example, answers different questions than does a history course. Turn to the next clean page in your journal, and title it "BEAUTIFUL ACADEMIC QUESTIONS." On that page, list the courses you're taking this semester, starting with this one. Leave five blank lines under each course. Following each course, put the three most important questions you think the course is designed to answer.* [10 minutes]

3. [Lead a discussion in which students share the questions they think various courses are designed to answer. Ask for students who are taking the same courses to compare their questions.]

4. [Journal Writing and/or Class Discussion] *What advantage is it for you to know what the key questions are for all your courses? How would you go about determining what questions a teacher might ask on a test? What do you think makes one question more beautiful than another? What is the life lesson here?* [e.g., If I ask the wrong question, I might get the "right" answer but it won't be much help to me.] [10–20 minutes]

Approximate Time: 50–60 minutes

Instructor Notes:
1. I like to make the point that the root word of *question* is "quest." Often, then, the quality of any quest is determined by the quality of the question that starts it.

Journal 24.   Learning to Make Course Corrections

EXERCISE 24-1: Course Corrections

Purpose: To identify self-defeating patterns and limiting beliefs that get students off course in challenging college courses.

Supplies and Setup: Making Course Corrections (next page); students in pairs [A & B]

Directions:
1. *Decide which of your present college courses is the most challenging for you. Then complete each of the thirteen sentences as it relates to your challenging course. For example, if your most challenging course this semester is Math 110, you'd write "1. So far in Math 110, I've been absent four times." Obviously, to get value from this exercise, you must be honest.* [10 minutes]

2. *Partner A, read your completed sentences to Partner B. Afterwards, Partner B, tell your partner any behavior, beliefs, or attitudes you heard that might limit his or her success. Where possible, suggest more empowering behaviors, beliefs, or attitudes that your partner could choose.* [10 minutes] *Now switch roles, and repeat the same process.* [10 minutes]

3. [Journal Writing and/or Class Discussion] *Are there any changes you intend to make in your behaviors, beliefs, or attitudes? What is the life lesson here?* [e.g., If I don't notice when I am off course and make a course correction, then I am my own worst enemy.] [5–10 minutes]

Approximate Time: 20–30 minutes

Making Course Corrections

Fill in the blank below with the name of a current college course that is the most challenging for you. Then complete the following sentences, letting your Inner Guide tell the truth here.

So far in _____ . . .
                  (course name)

1. I've been absent _____ times.

2. I've been late _____ times.

3. I've studied for this course an average of _____ hours per week.

4. I've completed _____ percent of the assignments.

5. I've done my work at _____ percent of my best effort.

6. I've participated actively in _____ percent of the classes I've attended.

7. I've attended _____ study group meetings.

8. I've attended _____ conferences with my instructor.

9. I've gotten tutoring _____ times this semester.

10. If I keep doing what I've been doing, the grade I'll probably get in this course is _____.

11. The advantages of my doing well in this course are . . .

12. The disadvantages of my doing poorly in this course are . . .

13. Changes I will make to improve my results in this course are . . .

EXERCISE 24-2: Changing Test-Taking Habits

Purpose: To discover new test-taking strategies for maximizing learning in college.

Supplies and Setup: Students in groups of 4 to 5, each with pen and paper

Directions:
1. *Most students have developed at least some strategies to help them do well on tests. In your group, discuss your favorite study strategies, and later a reporter will share some of your group's best ideas with the whole class. You won't know who the group reporter is until I call on you, so everyone needs to record all suggestions. Here are a few example strategies:*
   A. *Before a test, I copy my study notes onto smaller and smaller pieces of paper. Using abbreviations, symbols, and acronyms, I eventually reduce my notes to a piece of paper the size of a postage stamp. Then I memorize the notes on the postage stamp, throw it away, and I'm ready for the test.*
   B. *During a test, I skip the hard questions and come back to them last. This way I earn all the points available for easy questions. Your goal today is to come up with a list of great ways to do well on tests. Any questions? Okay, begin.* [5-10 minutes]
2. *Now let's have the recorders report each group's best ideas.* [As you write the ideas on the chalkboard or on an overhead transparency, you may want to have a student recorder make a copy that could later be copied and distributed. Consider grouping strategies into categories of before, during, and after the test.] [5–10 minutes]
3. [Freewriting and/or Class Discussion] *Which of these ideas will you try for your next test? Why?* [5–15 minutes]

Approximate Time: 20–30 minutes

Instructor Notes:
1. When students later look at "Wise Choices for Effective Studying" and "Wise Choices for Effective Test Taking," you can bring back their list to see how many of the strategies from *On Course* they named.

Journal 25. Developing Wisdom

EXERCISE 25-1: Choice-Evaluation Process

Purpose: To gain wisdom from a past mistake or a broken commitment.

Supplies and Setup: The six steps of the Choice-Evaluation Process (see Instructor Notes) written on the chalkboard or printed on a handout; students (A & B) sitting in pairs; journals

Directions:
1. *Everyone makes mistakes. Victims rarely learn anything from their mistakes; they also keep making them over and over. Creators, on the other hand, learn from their mistakes, and they seldom repeat the same mistake. This is one of the best ways that Creators become wise.*
2. *Before we do this activity, let's define a mistake. What do you think a mistake is?* [A definition I like is "A mistake is a choice that gets us off course from our dreams when a choice existed that could have kept us on course to our dreams." This definition keeps the Inner Critic at bay. After discussing the definition of a mistake, you might share a couple of mistakes that you have made in your life to get the students thinking about the mistakes they have made.] [5 minutes]

3. *Now I'd like you to recall a mistake that you have made in your life. Write it in your journal.* [Pause for a minute or 2.] *Have you all thought of at least one mistake that you've made in your life?* [3 minutes]

4. *The Choice-Evaluation Process is a technique for becoming more conscious of our mistakes and using them as valuable teachers. Now Partner A will use the Choice-Evaluation Process to do a self-examination of the mistake. When Partner A has done all six steps, Partner B, use your best active listening skills to tell Partner A what you heard. Here's what this might look like.* [Do a DEMO of the process using one of your own mistakes.] *Partner A, you will have five minutes. I'll let you know when the five minutes are up, and then you'll switch roles. Any questions? Ready, begin.* [You might want to ask at 5 minutes if anyone needs more time. When they are ready, have them switch roles and repeat the process.] [10–15 minutes]

5. [Journal Writing and/or Class Discussion] *What life lesson did you you learn from your mistake?* [*e.g.,* Sometimes I make choices based on what is convenient at the time rather than on what is best for accomplishing my goals.] [10–20 minutes]

Approximate Time: 30–45 minutes

Instructor Notes:
1. You'll notice that the Choice-Evaluation Process is similar to the Wise-Choice Process. While the Wise-Choice Process helps students make a wise choice in the *future*, the Choice-Evaluation Process helps them examine a *past* choice and 1) discover more supportive options and 2) learn an important life lesson (so they don't repeat a self-sabotaging choice in the future). If students have difficulty coming up with an answer for Step 1 (regarding a questionable choice), they can often find one by revisiting their answers to "Making Course Corrections" on Page 74. Or you might provide a questionable choice that you have seen the student make: "I notice you've been absent five times already this semester."

2. Here are the six steps of the Choice-Evaluation Process:
    1. What questionable choice (perhaps a mistake) did I make?
    2. Is this choice helping or hindering me to get what I want? (If "hindering," go on.)
    3. What other choices could I have made?
    4. What's the likely outcome of each choice?
    5. Which choice(s) will I commit to for the future?
    6. What's the life lesson for me here?

   To deepen the exploration of the life lesson (Step 6), you might ask additional questions:
   What did you make more important than choosing the better option originally?
   (Here we're looking to clarify values—conscious or unconscious.)
   Is that really a value you want dictating your choices?
   Can you see other times in your life when you have made a similar choice?
   (Here we're looking for a possible self-defeating pattern or script.)

3. A variation of the Choice-Evaluation Process creates valuable lessons from a broken commitment. This is particularly appropriate if you had your students create course commitments earlier in the semester. The only change is in Step 1.
    1. What commitment did I break?
    2. (Continue with Steps 2–6 above.)

EXERCISE 25-2: The Failure Toss

Purpose: To gain wisdom from a failure.

Supplies and Setup: Pen and paper for each student; trash can; students in groups of 5

Directions:

1. *Everyone has failed at something. Victims rarely learn anything from their failures; they may even keep having the same failure over and over. Creator, on the other hand, learn from their failures, and they seldom repeat them. This is another way that Creators become wise.* [1 minute]

2. *Before we do this activity, let's define a "failure." What do you think a failure is?* [A definition I like is "A failure is what your Inner Critic calls those times when you didn't create your goals or dreams exactly on schedule." This definition keeps the Inner Critic at bay. After discussing the definition of a failure, you might share a couple of your own failures to get the students thinking about ones they have had.] [5 minutes]

3. *Now I'd like you to fold your sheet of paper in half vertically, creating two columns. At the top of the left-hand column, write the word* FAILURES. *Below that, write a list of your failures in school and in life. No one else is going to see your failures, so you can be totally honest with yourself. Number each failure.* [5 minutes]

4. *At the top of the right-hand column, write the word* WISDOM. *In that column, write the valuable wisdom you learned from each of your failures. For example, maybe failure #1 was "My first marriage ended after only eight months." Next to that you might write that wisdom #1 was "I learned that I can never took to someone else to create my sense of security." Add as many wisdoms as you learned from each failure.* [5–10 minutes]

5. *Choose someone in your group to read one wisdom. Then keep going around your group clockwise, with each person reading one wisdom. Don't mention how you learned the wisdom, just state it. Keep going around your group until all in your group have presented all of their wisdoms or until I call time.* [5 minutes]

6. *Now tear your paper in half along the fold. This leaves you with your FAILURES in one hand and your WISDOMS in the other. Now make a choice. You can . . .*
   1. *Keep both your FAILURES and your WISDOMS.*
   2. *Throw away your FAILURES and keep your WISDOMS.*
   3. *Throw away your WISDOMS and keep your FAILURES.*
   4. *Throw away both your FAILURES and your WISDOMS.*
   Make that choice and do it now. If you choose to throw anything away, toss it into the trash can. [3 minutes]

7. [Journal Writing and/or Class Discussion] *what choice did you make? Why? What is the life lesson here?* [e.g., Every failure can be a powerful teacher.] [10–20 minutes]

Approximate Time: 25–35 minutes

Instructor Notes:

1. As a variation, you can have students title the left-hand column with any or all of these: Failures, Mistakes, Challenges, Obstacles, Adversities.

EXERCISE 25-3: Lessons from Your Obstacle

Purpose: To gain wisdom from an obstacle.

Supplies and Setup: Journals; chime; You may wish to play relaxing instrumental music during this activity

Directions:

1. *First, we're going to do a relaxation. Then, I am going to take you on a journey in your minds. So get comfortable in your chairs, close your eyes, and prepare to relax.* [Do a progressive relaxation technique such as the one found in Chapter 1 of *On Course*.] [5 minutes]

2. [After the relaxation, begin reading the following guided visualization, waiting about 10 seconds for any ellipses . . . and waiting about 20–30 seconds at a PAUSE.] *Now, in your mind, imagine that you are walking along a path at the foot of a majestic mountain . . . notice all the natural beauty that is around you . . . See the tall, green trees . . . Hear the birds warbling . . . Smell the wonderful piney odor . . . Feel the soft grass beneath your feet . . . Now look up at the top of the mountain. There in the distance at the top of the mountain see one of your most important dreams. Get a clear picture of your goal waiting for you at the top of this beautiful mountain. Picture your dream clearly and exactly as it will look when you have achieved it.* [PAUSE] *Now notice that there is a path that leads from where you are now, a path that goes all the way up the mountain to your dream . . . As your eyes follow the path up, notice any challenging obstacle on your path to your dream: perhaps the obstacle is a person in your way . . . perhaps it is a health problem . . . or not enough time . . . or lack of money . . . Perhaps your obstacle is a self-defeating behavior pattern like procrastination, or substance abuse, or watching too much television . . . Perhaps it is a self-defeating thought pattern like negative self-talk, self-judgments, or self-criticism . . . Perhaps it is self-defeating emotional patterns like constant anger or sadness or depression . . . Or perhaps it is a limiting belief about yourself, about other people, or about the world . . . What is the biggest, most challenging obstacle standing in the way to your dream? What does it look like? Picture it clearly now.* [PAUSE] *What if your obstacle could talk to you? What would it say to you? Take time right now to really listen to your obstacle . . . Listen for one sentence of advice from your obstacle . . . What lesson does your obstacle have to teach you? Listen now.* [PAUSE] *When you are ready, bring your awareness back to this room and open your eyes. In your journals, write any advice that your obstacle gave you.* [10 minutes]

3. [Have half of the students stand and move their chairs/desks to the edges of the room. This will leave half of the students sitting down with enough space between their chairs for the others to walk.]

4. *In a moment, those of you who are standing are going to whisper the wise advice your obstacle gave you to the people sitting.* [DEMO—for example, "You would be happier and more successful if you got away from people who constantly criticize you." Whisper this advice into 1 student's ear, and the move on and repeat the same advice to another student, and another.] *As soon as you have whispered your obstacle's advice to one person, move on to another person and whisper it again, and then move to another and another. If two of you arrive at the same person, you can both whisper into different ears. What could be better than great advice in stereo! There will be enough time for you to whisper your advice to everyone at least two times before I ring the chime* [or announce "reverse roles"]. [5 minutes]

5. *When you hear the chime, reverse places. Those of you sitting will stand, and those of you standing will sit. The people now standing will begin whispering their obstacle's wise advice in the ears of the people now sitting. Keep whispering the same advice to different people until you hear the chime a second time. Then find a seat and think about the wisdom you've just heard from your obstacle and the obstacles of others. Feel free to write any of this wisdom in your journal. Are there any questions?* [The success of this activity requires that everyone understand the directions before beginning, so be extra sure everyone is ready.] *Ready, begin.* [3 minutes]

6. [Let the first round of whispered advice go for about 2 minutes. Ring the chime to signal reversing roles and allow about 2 more minutes for the second round. Then ring the chime a last time and give students a few minutes to relax and take in the wisdom they have heard. [7 minutes]

7. [Freewriting/Discussion] *What was that experience like for you? What wisdom did you hear from your obstacle? From other people's obstacles? What is the life lesson here?* [e.g., I have a powerful Inner Guide, but I need to take the time to heed its wisdom.] [10–20 minutes]

Approximate Time: 40–50 minutes

Instructor Notes:
1. This activity sets up the Affirmation Whisper activity later in the course. The Affirmation Whisper—one of my students' favorites—will be even more powerful with this preparation.

Case Study for Critical Thinking: A Fish Story

Purpose: To use critical thinking skills to practice extracting valuable lessons from every experience, thus developing a key skill used by lifelong learners.

Supplies and Setup: "A Fish Story" in *On Course*; journals; chime

Directions:
1. [Have students read "A Fish Story." One way to be sure everyone has read the selection before taking the next step is to have 1 student read the first paragraph aloud, another student read the second, and so on until the reading is complete. [5 minutes]

2. *In your journal, write an answer to the first question at the bottom of the story: If you had been in this biology lab class, what lessons about college and life would you have learned from the experience?* [5 minutes]

3. [Put students in pairs with an A & B] *A, read to your partner the lessons you learned about college and life. B, you'll respond with your best active listening skills, reflecting what you heard and asking for clarification or expansion. When I ring the chime, change roles: B reads, and A is the active listener.* [5–10 minutes]

4. [Have A's switch partners, creating new pairs, and repeat Step 3 with their new partners. Switch and repeat Step 3 as often as time allows.] [5–25 minutes]

5. *Look at what you wrote originally and take a few minutes to see if you can now dive deeper. Write new insights you think you could have learned from the experience with the fish.* [5 minutes]

6. [Journal Writing and/or Class Discussion] *What did you learn from this discussion about extracting meaning from experience? What is the life lesson?* [e.g., The deeper I dive, the richer are the rewards.] [5–10 minutes]

Approximate Time: 25–55 minutes

Instructor Notes:
1. Point worth making: Human beings are "meaning makers." We have an experience, and then we make up what it means to us. We see the present experience through our past experience, and that shapes the meaning we make. Many "meanings" are embedded in any experience, and Creators seek the meaning that best supports their success. This will occasionally require them to revise their answers or beliefs about themselves, other people, or the world.

2. A variation is to have students write new insights and discoveries (Step 5) in their journals after each pair discussion.

Journal 26.   Developing Self-Respect

— **EXERCISE 26-1: Claiming Respect**

Purpose: To identify qualities that students respect in someone else and to own these projections.

Supplies and Setup: Journals; students sitting in pairs (A & B). Write the following sentence stem on the chalkboard or on an overhead transparency: **I respect _____ because . . .**

Directions:
1. *In your journal, write the name of a person for whom you have great respect. This person can be a family member, a co-worker, a friend, someone here at college, someone famous you haven't ever met . . . absolutely anyone you respect.* [2 minutes]
2. *Below the person's name, copy the sentence stem from the chalkboard:* **I respect (person's name) because . . .** *Then complete the sentence five or more times, giving a different reason each time for why you respect that person. Focus on HOW the person lives his or her life rather than his or her accomplishments. For example, I might write, "I respect my sister Holly because she has experienced a great deal of pain in her life, yet she remains one of the most loving and caring people I know." [5–8 minutes]*
3. *Partner A, read your sentences to Partner B. But when you read the sentence, you're going to substitute* **yourself** *for the person you originally wrote about. So, I would say, "I respect* **myself** *because* **I** *have experienced a great deal of pain in* **my** *life, yet* **I** *remain one of the most loving and caring people I know." Partner B, when your partner has read all the sentences, reflect what you heard him or her say. Partner A, be aware of any thoughts or feelings you have as you read.* [8–10 minutes]
4. *Switch roles. Partner B, you read now, and remember to substitute yourself for the person you originally wrote about. Afterwards, Partner A, reflect what you heard your partner say. And Partner B, remember to be aware of any thoughts or feelings you have as you read.* [8–10 minutes]
5. *[Freewriting/Discussion] Did you find that what you respect in the other person is a quality you have as well? What was it like to claim the respect for yourself that you also have for the other person? Did your Inner Critic have anything to say? How do you feel right now? What would it do for your self-confidence if you acknowledged respect for* **how** *you live your life? What is the life lesson here? [e.g., My level of self-respect is determined not only by the goals I achieve but also by how I achieve them.] [10–20 minutes]*

Approximate Time: 40–50 minutes

Instructor Notes:
1. You may wish to point out that we often project our own thoughts onto others. So respecting someone for a particular quality suggests we either have or want to have that same quality. Emphasize that self-respect is about having admiration for HOW we or others live life.

EXERCISE 26-2: Symbol of Self-Respect

Purpose: To acknowledge and express self-respect.

Supplies and Setup: Set up this activity in a previous class by requesting that students bring in an item of which they're proud. This item might be a sports trophy, a grade report, a scholarship letter, a wedding ring, a picture they painted, and so on. If they can't bring it the item, they can bring a photo or a sketch of it, or they can describe it to the class. Write two sentence stems on the chalk-board or on an overhead transparency: **I am proud of this item because . . . What this item reveals about how I live my life is . . .** Students in groups of 3.

Directions:

1. *The people who go first in each group will show the item they brought and (if necessary) explain what it is. Next, speaking to your group, complete the two sentence stems on the chalk-board. After the first person has gone, move clockwise around your group until everyone has finished.* [5–10 minutes]
2. *Now we are going to do the same exercise again. This time, go to your very deepest level of honesty. Let your Inner Guide suggest the deepest truth about why you are proud of this item and what it reveals about you. If you are proud of this item, it suggests a very deep self-respect. Honor yourself by expressing that deep self-respect.* [5–10 minutes]
3. [Freewriting/Discussion] *What was it like to tell about what you deeply respect about your-self? What thoughts or feelings did you have as you explained yourself each time? Did your Inner Critic try to interfere? How do you feel right now? What would it do for your self-esteem if you fully acknowledge your self-respect? What is the life lesson here?* [e.g., All of my accom-plishments are a window into my soul, revealing not only what is important to me but also how I live my life.] [10–20 minutes]

Approximate Time: 20–40 minutes

Instructor Notes:

1. Emphasize that self-respect is about having admiration for HOW we live our lives.

CHAPTER 7: Quiz Questions

23. Discovering Your Preferred Learning Style

1. The first step in the natural process of learning is to _____.
2. The second step in the natural process of learning is to _____.
3. The third step in the natural process of learning is to _____.
4. Knowing our learning style lets us understand how we prefer to learn. TRUE FALSE
5. If an instructor does not teach to our preferred learning style, we can never learn the information of that course. TRUE FALSE

Answers: 1. ask Creator questions 2. gather relevant information 3. discover empowering answers 4. TRUE 5. FALSE

24. Learning to Make Course Corrections

1. If your present habit patterns and beliefs aren't keeping you on course, you'll have to make a course _____.
2. The first step of course correction is to _____.
3. The second step of course correction is to _____.
4. The third step of course correction is to _____.
5. In order to course correct, one must have the courage to change. TRUE FALSE

Answers: 1. correction 2. test your present answers 3. heed feedback 4. revise your answers 5. TRUE

25. Developing Wisdom

1. In *On Course*, wisdom is defined as the deep and profound understanding that allows us to consistently make wise _____ that move us steadily and contentedly toward the creation of a life worth living.
2. Psychologist Martin Seligman says that people quit when they believe that the causes of their failures are permanent, pervasive, and _____.
3. Our Inner Guide knows that failure is merely feedback.   TRUE   FALSE
4. "Why do I always screw up?" is a likely response to failure by a person's _____.
   A. Inner Critic
   B. Inner Defender
   C. Inner Guide
5. Feeling helpless, according to psychologist Martin Seligman, is something that people are born with.   TRUE   FALSE

Answers: 1. choices 2. personal 3. TRUE 4. A 5. FALSE (Helplessness, he says, is learned.)

26. Developing Self-Respect

1. If self-confidence is the result of *what* I do, then self-respect is the result of _____ I do it.
2. Once we have a foundation of personal values, we create integrity by choosing words and actions consistent with those values.   TRUE   FALSE
3. Each time you make a choice that goes against your own values, you make a deposit in your self-respect account.   TRUE   FALSE
4. When you break a promise (especially to yourself), you make a withdrawal from your self-respect account.   TRUE   FALSE
5. Which of the following does not help you to keep commitments?
   A. Make your agreements unconsciously.
   B. Make your agreements important—write them down.
   C. Create a plan; then do everything in your power to carry it out!
   D. If a problem arises or you change your mind, renegotiate.

Answers: 1. how 2. TRUE 3. FALSE 4. TRUE 5. A

CHAPTER 7: Essay Topics

1. Recall your favorite teacher or subject. With what you now know about learning styles, write an essay in which you explain why you liked this teacher or subject so much.
2. Students new to college are often stuck in old habit patterns that sabotage their academic success. In an essay for college freshmen, offer your suggestions for the most important behaviors, beliefs, and attitudes necessary for academic success. Suggest ways your readers could make a course correction if they need to. Use your own experience wherever possible.
3. In an essay for members of your local board of education, write an evaluation of the quality of the education you received in high school. Make suggestions on how the education you received could be improved for those who follow you.
4. Educational philosopher John Dewey wrote, "The most important attitude that can be formed is that of the desire to go on learning." In an essay for new parents, discuss what they can do to preserve and nurture their children's love of learning.

5. Taking a personal inventory is often the first step toward improving an area of one's life. Write an essay in which you explore your strengths and weaknesses as a learner (both in school and out of school). End your essay by proposing changes that you could make to become a more effective learner.

6. Psychologist Mihaly Csikszentmihalyi wrote, "The ability to persevere despite obstacles and setbacks is the quality people most admire in others. . . ." Your perseverance through difficulties not only causes others to respect you, it raises your own self-respect. In an essay for a general audience, describe a time in your life when you persevered against inner and/or outer obstacles to reach a goal or dream of great importance to you. Conclude by telling what you learned from your experience and how it affected your sense of self-respect.

Chapter 8
Developing Emotional Intelligence

Concept

People in the grip of overwhelming emotions are typically ineffective. Consequently, one of the most essential components of success—by some accounts more important than academic intelligence—is emotional intelligence. Emotional intelligence is the ability to manage one's emotions and stay on course even when navigating life's most challenging storms. Just as we are responsible for the quality of our outer life, we are responsible for the quality of our inner life as well. In fact, cognitive psychologists suggest that we can only perceive what is going on outside of us through the lens of what is going on inside of us. Our inner conversations create our interpretation of the events going on around us, and in this way, our thoughts actually create our "reality." People who are emotionally intelligent are skilled at controlling the content of their consciousness. This skill allows them to make wise choices, while others struggle merely to survive their emotional storms. When we assist students to gain greater emotional intelligence, we empower them not only to be more effective in the pursuit of their dreams, but also to experience happiness, joy, and peace of mind on their journey.

Empowers Students to . . .

1. Take responsibility for the quality of their inner experience of life.
2. Honor their emotions, seeing both pleasant and unpleasant emotions as important feedback for keeping them on course.
3. More consciously choose the content of their consciousness, thinking and speaking more positively about themselves, others, and their world, thus creating an experience of greater optimism, joy, and happiness.
4. Avoid emotional hijackings, thus persisting in the face of challenges and setbacks.
5. Learn how to create more "flow" or peak experiences in their lives, both at work and at play.
6. Improve relationships through empathy for and an understanding of the emotions of others.
7. Postpone instant gratification for a later, greater reward.

Remember to consider using the all-purpose exercises mentioned in the introduction, especially JOURNAL READINGS, QUOTATIONS, POEMS, CARTOONS, FOCUS QUESTIONS, AND CHAPTER-OPENING SUMMARIES. Remind students to use letters to label any in-class writing they do in their journals.

Journal 27. Understanding Emotional Intelligence

EXERCISE 27-1: I'm Willing to Feel . . .

Purpose: To help students become more conscious of the emotions they accept and those they reject.

Supplies and Setup: Students in pairs (A & B). Write the list of "I'm willing . . ." statements on the chalkboard or project on an overhead transparency screen. [See Instructor Notes for list.]

Directions:

1. *Healthy emotions tell us when we're on course or off course. Most people were raised to be comfortable with some emotions but uncomfortable with others. This exercise is designed to help you become more conscious of how comfortable you are with various emotions.* [2 minutes]

2. *Partner A will read one of the "I'm willing . . ." statements. Partner B will respond, "I can accept you when you are feeling _____."* [Fill in the emotion that Partner A has just mentioned.] *Each of you, be conscious of how you feel as you say your part.* [DEMO the process.] *You may find that you feel comfortable when you express anger but uncomfortable when your partner expresses anger. Just be sensitive to how you feel as you say or listen to each of these statements about feeling your emotions. Watch for any changes in your body, like a flutter in your stomach, as you say or hear one of these sentences. If you finish before I call time, go back to the top of the list and repeat the list. Any questions? Okay, Partner A, begin.* [5 minutes]

3. *Now switch roles. Partner B, you read the statement, and Partner A responds, "I can accept you when you are feeling _____." Again, the key here is to be aware of how you feel as you express these ideas.* [3 minutes]

4. [Freewriting/Class Discussion] *What emotions are you comfortable with feeling? Uncomfortable with feeling? What emotions are you comfortable with others feeling? Uncomfortable with others feeling? What do you suppose is the value for you of this awareness? What is the life lesson here?* [e.g., My emotions show up in my body long before they show up in my mind.] [5–20 minutes]

Approximate Time: 15–35 minutes

Source: This is a variation of an exercise by authors Gay and Kathlyn Hendricks.

Instructor Notes: Here are the statements to put on the chalkboard or overhead transparency:

1. I'm willing to feel all of my overwhelm.
2. I'm willing to feel all of my anger.
3. I'm willing to feel all of my anxiety.
4. I'm willing to feel all of my fear.
5. I'm willing to feel all of my sadness.
6. I'm willing to feel all of my guilt.
7. I'm willing to feel all of my resentment.
8. I'm willing to feel all of my depression.
9. I'm willing to feel all of my love.
10. I'm willing to feel all of my joy.

EXERCISE 27-2: Right Now I Feel . . .

Purpose: To improve students' ability to be aware of their emotions and to dramatize how the words we think affect how we feel.

Supplies and Setup: Students in groups of 3. Write the list of sentence stems on the chalkboard or project on an overhead transparency screen. [See Instructor Notes for the sentence stems.]

Directions:
1. *For many people, staying in touch with their feelings is a great challenge. This exercise is designed to assist us to become more aware of our feelings.*
2. *Before we start, let's list as many feelings as we can think of. Call them out.* [Record the list of emotions on the chalkboard, calling out suggestions that are not really feelings, such as "stupid." "Stupid" is not a feeling, but "embarrassed" is. Discuss distinctions between emotions such as fear and anxiety, sadness and depression, anger and fury.]
3. *The person with the shortest hair in your group will go first. That person will read and complete the first sentence stem. Moving clockwise, the other two people will read and complete the same sentence. Then the first person will read and complete the second sentence, and so on until all the sentences have been read and completed by each person. Be very conscious of both how you feel and how it feels to say how you feel.* [DEMO the process.] *Any questions? Okay, decide who will go first, and begin.* [5–8 minutes]
4. [Freewriting/Class Discussion] *What did you learn about your relationship to the various emotions you discussed? Did you notice your emotions changing as you read about the various emotions? What does this suggest about ways to manage our emotions? What is the life lesson here?* [e.g., The thoughts that I allow to linger in my mind determine the emotions that show up in my heart.] [5–20 minutes]

Approximate Time: 10–30 minutes

Instructor Notes:
1. Here are the statements to put on the chalkboard or overhead transparency:

   Right now I feel . . .
   I feel angry when . . .
   I feel afraid when . . .
   I feel sad when . . .
   Right now I feel . . .
   I feel calm when . . .
   I feel peaceful when . . .
   I feel contented when . . .
   Right now I feel . . .
   I feel happy when . . .
   I feel joyful when . . .
   I feel loved when . . .
   Right now I feel . . .

2. An important point to bring out in the discussion is that the thoughts we allow in our consciousness greatly influence how we feel. Typically, reading the words about an emotion causes the emotion. These stems are set up to move students from negative emotions to tranquil emotions to positive emotions.
3. A variation is to have students write and complete sentence stems (instead of speaking them). In this way they will create a kind of poem about their emotions.

Journal 28. Reducing Stress

EXERCISE 28-1: Up on the Roof

Purpose: To experience how changing the content of one's consciousness changes the quality of one's experience.

Directions:
1. *I'd like you to stand up and position yourself so you can spread your arms without touching anyone else. In a moment, I'm going to invite you to close your eyes, and I'm going to guide you through a mental experience with words. Try to totally involve yourself in the experience, and see if you don't discover a wonderful truth about life. When you're ready, close your eyes, take a deep breath, and here we go.* [1 minute]
2. *Picture yourself walking along a sidewalk in a large city. Above you, tall buildings tower as you weave your way through the crowd on the sidewalk. Now you come to a huge building with a revolving door. As you push on the glass door, it glides open, and you find yourself entering an expansive lobby. Walk across the smooth marble floor to the elevator and push the UP button. The doors open, and once inside the empty elevator, you push the top button marked "ROOF." Hear the elevator music, and then feel the light sensation in your stomach as the elevator begins rushing you upward. After a long ride, the elevator doors open, and you step out into a deserted hallway. Look down at the end of the hall . . . notice a door down there. Walk over to the door, turn the handle, and push the door open. Now step into the dimly light stairway. Take the stairs up until you come to the second door. Push on the horizontal bar and feel the latch opening and the door swinging open. The brightness of the sun causes you to squint your eyes, and the breeze blows across you as you step out onto the crunchy gravel of the roof. Birds are flying overhead, and the sky is dotted with a few white clouds. Notice that the edge of the building has a little parapet, a one-foot-high cement wall that runs around the entire roof. Walk over to the parapet, once again feeling the strong breeze brushing your face and hair. As you reach the parapet, step up on it. That's right—lift your foot and step right up on that little wall that runs around the very edge of the roof. Look over into the canyon between the buildings . . . notice the tiny people way down below . . . listen to the far-off sounds of automobile horns honking in the city . . . Now, see how far out over the edge you can lean, and be aware of how you are feeling as you lean over that open space below you. . . . Be careful! That breeze is blowing mighty hard. Don't let it blow you over the edge. . . . Okay, now step back down to the roof, feeling the gravel crunch beneath your shoes once again.* [5 minutes]
3. *Now as you stand on the roof, an amazing thing begins to happen. You feel a tingle on your back. Something is growing out of each of your shoulder blades. In a moment you realize that wings are coming right through your clothing, and they keep growing until they are large and strong. Strangely, these wings feel very familiar to you, as if you have had them all of your life. Flap your wings a few times. Notice that you have full control of them. Feel yourself confidently lift off of the roof a few feet, then settle back down. Now that you have your wings, and you feel confident in their use, step back up on the little parapet, the cement wall running around the edge of the roof. Once again, feel the wind blowing at your back, see the birds flying overhead, and look down at the tiny people and cars far below. Try leaning out again, and this time, if you want, let yourself soar off of the roof and fly around with the birds high into the white clouds. Soar around as high as you wish to go, then, after an exhilarating flight, come back and land once again on the roof. Step off the parapet and feel the gravel again beneath your shoes. In a*

moment, I'll be inviting you to open your eyes and return to this room, but before you do, you have something to decide. You need to decide if you will bring your wings back here with you or leave them behind. So, when you have decided whether or not to keep your wings, take a deep breath, let your eyes come open, and have a seat. [5 minutes]

4. [Freewriting/Class Discussion] *What did you experience when you stepped up on the parapet for the first time?* [Some people will report fear or concern about being on the roof.] *Was your experience different when you got your wings?* [Many people will report a much more positive experience once they got their wings.] *How many of you had a more positive experience on the roof after you got your wings? Where did your wings come from?* [They created them with their thoughts.] *What is the life lesson about how to create a more positive experience of life?* [By consciously choosing to occupy the content of our consciousness with positive thoughts, we change our experience of life for the better. We can reduce stress by changing our thoughts.] *What is an area of your life where you could apply this wisdom?* [10–20 minutes]

Approximate Time: 20–30 minutes

Instructor Notes:
1. This visualization can lead to some great discoveries. After this visualization, one participant said, "Thanks for reminding me that I have wings and that I can fly." You might even want to follow the activity by playing the song "I Believe I Can Fly" by R. Kelly.

EXERCISE 28-2: Resolving Incompletions

Purpose: To give participants the stress-reducing experience of an outer world completion.

Supplies and Setup: Step 1 is done in one class period; Step 2 is done in the following class period.

Directions:
1. *Open your journal to a blank page. Make a list of incompletions that exist in your outer world, things you have been meaning to do but keep putting off. For example, you might include incompletions such as (1) make a dentist appointment, (2) get my car tuned, (3) tell my boyfriend that I am upset with him, (4) complete term paper for history. Circle one of these incompletions that you are willing to complete before our next class meeting. Now I'd like each person to announce what he or she is going to complete. You'll get to report your results in our next class.* [Allow students to "pass" on the announcement if they want.] [10 minutes]
2. [Next class period] [Freewriting/Class Discussion] *What did you promise yourself to complete? How successful were you? How do you feel right now about completing or not completing it? If you didn't complete the action, what did you make more important than doing it? Does your Inner Critic or Inner Defender have anything to say about your failure to complete it? Are you willing to recommit to doing it? What is the life lesson here?* [e.g., Resolving incompletions is a great way to reduce stress caused by feeling overwhelmed.] [10–30 minutes]

Approximate Time: 20–40 minutes [spread over two classes]

EXERCISE 28-3: Happy Music

Purpose: To demonstrate that what we choose as the content of our consciousness influences the quality of our experience.

Supplies and Setup: Audiotape or compact disc player. In the previous class, ask students to bring a song that inspires them or makes them feel happy, or the instructor can bring a variety of songs.

Directions:

1. [Invite volunteers to play their songs.] [3–5 minutes for each song]
2. [Freewriting/Class Discussion] *How do you feel right now? Do you feel better or worse than before you heard the music? What is it about the music that created this feeling? What is the life lesson about changing your emotional state?* [e.g., I can manage my emotions by making wise choices about the music I listen to . . . and the books I read . . . and the friends I have . . . and by all that I allow into my mind.] *How can you apply this idea in other ways besides music?* [5–10 minutes]

Approximate Time: 5–45 minutes [depending on how many songs you play]

Instructor Notes:

1. This is a good exercise to carry over to other class periods. You can begin or end a class with one or two uplifting songs.
2. This exercise is also a good diversity exercise, allowing students to hear the diverse music that inspires or makes their classmates happy.

Journal 29. Creating Flow

EXERCISE 29-1: Clump

Purpose: To offer participants an opportunity to explore their relationship with play. Note: This is a great energizer and mood lightener, too.

Supplies and Setup: Chairs pushed to the sides of the room; students standing in the middle of the room

Directions:

1. *We're going to play a very silly child's game called Clump. Be aware of what you tell yourself and how you feel both as I describe the game and as you play it. Here's the way to play Clump. First, everyone walks around the room. As you walk, I'll call out "Clump" and a number, such as "Clump 4." As soon as you hear "Clump 4," your goal is to grab hold of others to form a clump of four people, no more, no less. When I call "Freeze," everyone stops right where they are. Those not clumped in fours are out, just like in musical chairs. When you're "out," please sit down. Any questions? Okay, let the game of Clump begin.* [Vary the Clump number each time: Clump 2, Clump 6, Clump 3, and so on.] [5–10 minutes, depending on size of the group]
2. [Freewriting/Class Discussion] *What did you tell yourself when you heard how to play Clump? What did you tell yourself while you were playing? How did you feel while playing? How do you feel right now? Do you like to play? What kind of play do you like? Why do you suppose some people lose the urge to play as they grow older? What gets in their way? What might their Inner Critics or Inner Defenders have to say? Is there any change you'd like to make in your life regarding play? What is the life lesson here?* [e.g., Playing keeps me young at heart.] [5–10 minutes]

Approximate Time: 10–20 minutes

Instructor Notes:
1. Optional: Videotape a group of children playing Clump. Show the video and talk about the difference between the way the children and the adults played. Explore: Why the difference?
2. Be particularly sensitive to the people who don't want to participate in this playful activity. Ask them what their Inner Critic or Inner Defender is telling them. Note also that some people confuse play with competition: If there's no competition, there's no play. Help them ease these two concepts apart. Also, you may need to adapt the game to the physical limitations of some of your students.

EXERCISE 29-2: Work Becomes Play

Purpose: To explore how we can bring more of the advantages of play into our work.

Supplies and Setup: Chalkboard or overhead transparency. Students in groups of 4 to 5

Directions:
1. *What are the positive characteristics of play? What makes play fun and enjoyable?* [Make a list of answers on the chalkboard or overhead transparency. For example, ideas might include "Games allow you to start over often"; "You get to choose your teammates"; "You decide when to play"; "There are immediate rewards for your skills"; "Rules keep the players honest"; "It's exciting to compete"; "Winning is fun"; "Each time you play, you improve your skills."] [5–10 minutes]
2. [Assign each group a small number of the listed items to discuss.] *Your goal is to figure out how to have your present or future work take on the characteristics of play that are on your list. For example, if play offers immediate rewards for your skills, think of how you could experience that same characteristic in your work.* [10–15 minutes]
3. *Let's have a report from each group on some of your best ideas.* [10–15 minutes]
4. [Freewriting/Class Discussion] *Why do you suppose some people hate the work they do? What did you learn about enjoying work? How do you feel about the work you do now or plan to do in the future? Is there any change you'd like to make in your life regarding work? What is the life lesson here?* [e.g., I can make choices that make my work more like play.] [10–20 minutes]

Approximate Time: 25–35 minutes

Case Study for Critical Thinking: After Math

Purpose: To develop critical thinking skills by exploring a real-life situation that revolves around emotional intelligence.

Supplies and Setup: "After Math" in *On Course*

Directions:
1. [Have students read "After Math." One way to be sure everyone has read the selection before taking the next step is to have 1 student read the first paragraph aloud, another student read the second, and so on until the reading is complete. Then have students put in their scores for the 5 characters. You may want to review the 5 components of Emotional Intelligence so that students are making informed choices.] [5 minutes]
2. [Find out by a show of hands how many students have picked each character as number 5—least emotionally intelligent. If 2 or more characters are chosen as number 5, move on to Step 3. In the

unlikely event that everyone chooses the same character as number 5 (or there is otherwise little diversity in opinion), ask how many students have picked each character as number 1—most emotionally intelligent.] [3 minutes]

3. [Create groups of like-minded students.] *Since you agree in your group about which character has the least (or most) emotional intelligence, decide how you are going to persuade others to agree with you. Be sure to explain your opinion by making reference to the five components of Emotional Intelligence.* [5–10 minutes]

4. [Have a spokesperson from each group present the group's position; then lead a debate on the issue by moving the discussion from group to group, allowing students to explain their positions in more detail and rebut opposing views. Invite students to demonstrate a change in their opinion by getting up and going to the group with which they now agree. Insist on students' referring to the components of Emotional Intelligence to keep the discussion from wandering into idiosyncratic arguments.] [5–20 minutes]

5. [Create the role-play suggested in the "Diving Deeper" section. A student volunteer role-plays a student character in the story while another volunteer role-plays a mentor offering specific advice on how this student could better handle his or her emotions: Overwhelm, Anger, Anxiety, or Sadness. Finally, the mentor can guide the character to discover what valuable life lesson is available from this experience.] [5–15 minutes]

6. [Journal Writing and/or Class Discussion] *What did you learn from this discussion about emotional intelligence and its importance for achieving your goals and dreams? What is the life lesson here?* [e.g., If I manage my emotions, I will have a far better life than if I let my emotions manage me.] [5–10 minutes]

Approximate Time: 25–55 minutes

Instructor Notes:
1. So as not to stifle discussion, I don't tell students what my scores are.
2. This class discussion is an excellent prewriting activity to be followed by students writing a persuasion essay supporting their opinions in the debate. Because students are now sharply aware of views opposed to their own, they often write much more thorough and persuasive essays than would be the case without the debate.
3. You might ask students to relate an experience they have witnessed in which someone (perhaps themselves) became hijacked by emotions and tell what happened as a result. Afterwards, ask, "What could this person have done that would have been more emotionally intelligent?"

Journal 30.   Believing in Yourself: Develop Self-Love

EXERCISE 30-1: Ways to Love Myself

Purpose: To create dozens of options for treating oneself with love.

Supplies and Setup: Overhead transparency projector; 4 transparency pens; journals; 32-DAY COMMITMENT FORMS (see next page). Label 4 overhead transparencies with one each of the following words: PHYSICAL, MENTAL, EMOTIONAL, SPIRITUAL.

Directions:
1. *Some of us are better at loving other people than we are at loving ourselves. Sometimes that's because we're just not sure how to love ourselves; nobody ever taught us. So, today we're going to*

32-Day Commitment

Because I know that this commitment will keep me on course to my goals, I promise myself that every day for the next 32 days I will take the following action:

Day 1			Day 17	
Day 2			Day 18	
Day 3			Day 19	
Day 4			Day 20	
Day 5			Day 21	
Day 6			Day 22	
Day 7			Day 23	
Day 8			Day 24	
Day 9			Day 25	
Day 10			Day 26	
Day 11			Day 27	
Day 12			Day 28	
Day 13			Day 29	
Day 14			Day 30	
Day 15			Day 31	
Day 16			Day 32	

By making and keeping promises to ourselves and others, little by little, our honor becomes greater than our moods.

Stephen Covey

Success is . . . the long-term consequence of making and keeping promises—promises to others . . . and promises to yourself . . . the more you exercise your self-discipline, the stronger it gets.

Harvey Cook

create a list of ways we can be loving to ourselves. [Divide the class into 4 equal groups and give each group 1 of the overhead transparencies and a pen.] [3 minutes]

2. *Your group's goal is to come up with a list of at least twenty ways you can be loving to yourself in the realm you've been assigned. For example, what ways can you be loving to yourself **physi-cally**?* [Elicit ideas, such as get a massage, eat a healthy meal, etc.] *What ways can you be loving to yourself **mentally**?* [Listen to my Inner Guide and not my Inner Critic, read a good book, etc.] *What ways can you be loving to yourself **emotionally**?* [Spend time with people I love, express anger, etc.] *What ways can you be loving to yourself **spiritually**?* [Say a prayer, spend time in nature, etc.] *Write your ideas on the transparency.* [During the activity, you might want to assist any group that may get stuck.] [10 minutes]

3. *Now we're going to hear some great ideas for loving ourselves. In your journal, title a page WAYS TO LOVE MYSELF. I suggest that you make a list in your journal of all the suggestions, even the ones you don't think you'll ever do. When you're reading your journal five years from now, you may come across a suggestion that will be just perfect for you then. Now, let's have a reporter present each group's suggestions. Keep your presentation under five minutes.* [20 minutes]

4. *Here's a 32-Day Commitment form. I invite you to consider making a commitment to do one of these loving things for yourself every day for 32 days. Is there anyone who would like to publicly announce a 32-Day Commitment?* [5 minutes]

5. [Freewriting/Discussion] *What would your life be like if you treated yourself with these loving actions when you are going through a challenge or a crisis in your life? What would it do for your self-esteem if you treated yourself better every day? What is the life lesson here?* [e.g., If I consistently treat myself with love, I'll have plenty of overflow for the important people in my life.] [10–20 minutes]

Approximate Time: 45–55 minutes

Instructor Notes:

1. Students may disagree about the placement of some ideas for loving oneself (for example, does "Meditate" belong under Mental or Spiritual?). I allow items to stay wherever they are placed; if an item comes up in two or more realms, that's fine, too. The point is that students leave class with a menu of self-caring options.

EXERCISE 30-2: Affirmation Whisper

Purpose: To demonstrate the power of self-affirming statements and give students' self-worth a boost.

Supplies and Setup: Chime. Students need to know their personal affirmation (Journal Entry #10) by heart or have it written on a 3″ x 5″ card. Have half of the students stand and move their chairs/desks to the sides of the room. Leave space between the remaining chairs for the standing students to walk among the sitting students I recommend soothing instrumental music as background; "Angelic Music" by Iasos is my choice.

Directions:

1. *In a moment, those of you who are standing are going to whisper your affirmation in the ears of the people sitting down. But instead of saying, "I am a bold, happy, loving man," you will say "**You** are a bold, happy, loving . . . **man or woman**," whichever is appropriate. It helps also to*

say the person's name first. [DEMO by whispering your affirmation into 1 student's ear and then moving on and repeating it.] *As soon as you have whispered your affirmation to one person, move on to another person and whisper your affirmation again. If two of you arrive at a person simultaneously, you can both whisper your affirmation into different ears. Affirmations in stereo are great! There will be enough time for you to whisper your affirmation to everyone at least two or three times, so keep whispering until you hear the chime! And here's a last thought for those of you sitting down—it seems to enrich the experience if you close your eyes.* [5 minutes]

2. *When you hear the chime, reverse roles. Those of you sitting will stand, and those of you standing will sit. As before, the standing people will begin whispering their affirmations to the sitting people. You'll have time to get to everyone two or three times, so don't stop whispering until you hear the chime. This time when you hear the chime, find a comfortable position anywhere in the room, sitting or lying down, and take a few minutes to think and feel what that experience was like for you. Are there any questions?* [The success of this activity requires that everyone understands before beginning, so be extra sure everyone is clear about the directions.] *Ready, begin.* [Let the first round of whispered affirmations go for about 2 minutes. Ring the chime to signal reversing roles and allow about 2 more minutes for the second round. Then ring the chime a last time and give students about 5 minutes in silence to relax and take in the affirmations they have heard.] [8 minutes]

3. [Freewriting/Discussion] *What was that experience like for you? How do you feel right now? What can you do to feel like this more often? What did you hear? What is the life lesson here?* [*e.g.,* How different, warmer, sweeter this life might have been, if only once each day I might have heard these loving words so gently spoken.] [10–20 minutes]

Approximate Time: 20–40 minutes

Instructor Notes:
1. This powerful activity is one of my students' all-time favorites. It often creates an experience for some students that is nothing short of sacred; I take great precautions that no one ruins that experience for the class. Occasionally, there is someone who gets uncomfortable and wants to make a joke of the activity. If you sense there is someone in your class who might do this, give everyone the opportunity not to participate.

EXERCISE 30-3: What I Love About Myself

Purpose: To acknowledge lovable characteristics about oneself.

Supplies and Setup: Students sitting in pairs (A & B)

Directions:
1. *For the next little while, you're going to have an exchange with your partner about self-love. Whoever starts will say, "What I love about myself is . . ." and finish the sentence. Then the other person will say, "What I love about myself is . . ." and finish the sentence. Go back and forth. Take your time. Think deeply and feel deeply. Trust your Inner Guide and don't hold back.* [You might want to do a DEMO by sharing some of the things you love about yourself.] [5 minutes]

2. [Freewriting/Discussion] *What was that experience like for you? What was it like to hear your partner expressing love for him- or herself? What was it like to say what you love about your-*

self? What thoughts or feelings did you have as you expressed yourself each time? Did your Inner Critic try to interfere? How do you feel right now? What would it do for your self-esteem if you fully acknowledged all your lovable traits? What is the life lesson here? [e.g., Loving myself is the secret ingredient to my success.] [10–20 minutes]

Approximate Time: 15–25 minutes

Instructor Notes:
1. You might want to suggest that students choose a partner with whom they have felt a close connection during the semester. This closeness can free people to be more expressive of their loving for themselves.

CHAPTER 8: Quiz Questions

27. Employing Emotional Intelligence

1. Having mental intelligence is all one needs to create great success in college and in life.   TRUE FALSE
2–3. Two components of Emotional Intelligence include _____ and _____.
4–5. Two steps that will assist people to become more attuned to their emotions include _____ and
     _____.

Answers: 1. FALSE 2–3. Two of the following: Recognize our emotions as they occur. Manage our distressing emotions in a positive way. Control impulses and motivate ourselves. Recognize others' emotions (empathy). Handle feelings that come up in a relationship. 4–5. Two of the following: Build a vocabulary of feelings. Be mindful of emotions *as* they are happening. Understand what is causing your emotion. Recognize the difference between a feeling and resulting actions.

28. Reducing Stress

1. Creators know they are responsible not only for the results they create in their outer world but also for the emotions they generate in their inner world. TRUE FALSE
2. One strategy to keep from being overwhelmed by **anger** is _____.
3. One strategy to keep from being overwhelmed by **fear** is _____.
4. One strategy to keep from being overwhelmed by **sadness** is _____.
5. According to Victor Frankl, a psychiatrist who survived the Nazi concentration camps during World War II, everything can be taken away from a person except the freedom to choose one's

     _____.

Answers: 1. TRUE 2. Any of the following: Separate, exercise, relax, reframe, elevate, distract yourself, identify the hurt, forgive. 3. Any of the following: relax, breathe deeply, detach, reframe, visualize success with safety, assume the best, distract yourself, face the fear. 4. Any of the following: exercise, laugh, breathe deeply, do something toward your goals, challenge pessimistic beliefs, socialize with friends and loved ones, help others in need, focus on the positive, find the opportunity in the problem. 5. attitude

29. Creating Flow

1. When our perceived skill level is high and our perceived challenge level is low, our inner experience is one of _____.
2. When our perceived skill level is low and our perceived challenge level is high, our inner experience is one of _____.
3. When our perceived skill level and our perceived challenge level are about the same, our inner experience is one of _____.
4. Psychologist Mihaly Csikszentmihalyi found that typical working Americans experience the most flow _____.
   A. while watching television
   B. over the weekend
   C. away on vacations
   D. on their jobs
5. Recreation is a Quadrant IV (unimportant and nonurgent) action.   TRUE   FALSE

Answers: 1. boredom   2. anxiety   3. flow   4. D   5. FALSE (Re-creation is important!)

30. Believing in Yourself: Develop Self-Love

1. Self-love grows not only by *what* you do, it also grows by _____ as you do it.
2. Self-love empowers us to make wise, self-supporting choices instead of unconscious, self-destructive ones.   TRUE   FALSE
3. A complete self-care plan includes nurturing ourselves _____, mentally, emotionally, and spiritually.
4. One way to nurture yourself mentally is _____.
5. One way to nurture yourself emotionally is _____.

Answers: 1. how to treat yourself 2. TRUE 3. physically 4. Various answers possible. 5. Various answers possible.

CHAPTER 8: Essay Topics

1. Misfortune happens to every human being. Victims often get overwhelmed by their anger, fear, and sadness while Creators move on to more positive futures. Using your knowledge of Emotional Intelligence and strategies for reducing stress, write an essay comparing how you dealt with a misfortune in your past with how you might deal with it today.
2. Much research has been done on "flow" experiences in which time seems to stop and the participant is totally and positively absorbed in the activity. In an essay intended to contribute to a better understanding of "flow," offer a description of one of your own "flow" experiences at work or at play.
3. Few people are fully conscious of the chatter of their inner aspects such as their Inner Defender, Inner Critic, and Inner Guide. In an essay for college students, explain how these inner aspects will impact the quality of their inner experience. Present your readers with methods for dealing positively with their inner voices.
4. Author William Saroyan advised, "Try as much as possible to be wholly alive. . . . You will be dead soon enough." In an essay for a general audience, explain what specific steps one can take to create the experience of feeling "wholly alive."

5. Many people focus on what is wrong in their lives, while a rare few seem to radiate a positive outlook on life. In an essay for a mass circulation magazine (like *Reader's Digest*), write an essay in which you tell about the most positive person you have ever known.

6. We sense how much a person loves us by how he or she treats us, especially in times of challenge or pain. Similarly, we can know how much we love ourselves by how we treat ourselves both in good times and in bad times. Write an essay for teenagers who are addicted to drugs. In this essay describe the importance of self-love, offer ways to assess the level of one's self-love, and help these teenagers develop a self-care plan for increasing their self-love.

Chapter 9
Staying On Course to Your Success

Concept

Staying on course to a rich, personally fulfilling life is one of a human being's greatest challenges. Forces both outside of us and inside of us constantly conspire to divert us from this achievement. Perhaps the most consistent forces tugging us off course are found within our own life scripts—the self-defeating behaviors, thoughts, and emotions supported by the unconscious limiting core beliefs that long ago became our personal reality. Even when we become aware of these habit patterns and beliefs, we find it difficult to make permanent positive changes. Too often and too soon, we slip back into our old ways and find ourselves once more off course. By assisting students to take their next steps, we not only remind them of the changes they have made to better their lives, we help them keep their sights on both a positive future and the wise choices necessary to guide them there. As we bid our students farewell from this course, we give them the momentum to head off into life with their new, empowering choices consciously held and dearly guarded.

Empowers Students to . . .

1. Review what they have learned about themselves in this course.
2. Assess the changes they have made to improve the outcomes of their lives.
3. Identify additional life changes they wish to make in the near and distant future.
4. Plan their next steps toward living a rich, personally fulfilling life.

Journal 31. Planning Your Next Steps

EXERCISE 31-1: Self-Assessment

Purpose: To have students acknowledge the changes they have created in their lives during this course and to decide what additional changes they want to make.

Supplies and Setup: Journal #31 completed, perhaps in class. Students sitting in pairs (A & B)

Directions:
1. *Partner A, read to your partner what you wrote for Step 2 of Journal Entry #31. When Partner A is finished, Partner B will respond, "What I heard you saying in this entry is . . ." Partner B can then add any other comments or observations that come to mind. [5 minutes]*
2. *Now, Partner B, you read Step 2 of your Journal Entry #31. Afterwards, Partner A will respond, "What I heard you saying in this entry is . . ." and then add any other comments or observations that seem appropriate. [5 minutes]*
3. *[Repeat Steps 1 and 2 above for Step 3 of Journal #31.] [8–10 minutes for both partners to read and respond]*

4. [Repeat Steps 1 and 2 above for Step 4 of Journal #31.] [8–10 minutes for both partners to read and respond]

5. [Freewriting/Discussion] *What important discoveries have you made in this course? What changes have you made in our lives? What additional changes do you plan to make in the future? What life lessons do you want to remember from this course?* [10–20 minutes]

Approximate Time: 30–50 minutes

EXERCISE 31-2: Commencement

Purpose: To offer an opportunity for students to review what they have learned and then preview their desired future and how they are going to get there.

Supplies and Setup: A beach ball (or other light ball) with key terms written on it with a permanent marker: SELF-RESPONSIBILITY, SELF-MOTIVATION, SELF-MANAGEMENT, INTERDEPENDENCE, SELF-AWARENESS, LIFE-LONG LEARNING, EMOTIONAL INTELLIGENCE, BELIEVE IN YOURSELF, WISE CHOICES, STUDY SKILLS (and any other concepts you want to review). Write 4 sentence stems on the chalkboard or on an overhead transparency. [See Instructor Notes below for the sentence stems.] Paper and pens. Optional: video camera

Directions:
1. [You may wish to have students standing in a circle for this step.] *Let's take a few minutes to review where we've been this semester. I'm going to toss this ball to someone. When you catch it, read the first word or words that you see and tell us whatever comes to mind about that topic. You can tell us what the concept means to you or about a strategy you learned, an experience you had that illustrates this concept, or whatever feels appropriate to you. There is no right or wrong answer. When you're done, toss the ball to another person, and that person will do the same thing. Don't worry if you talk about the same words on the ball that someone else discussed. Each word will probably be discussed a number of times in different ways.* [10–15 minutes, or until you sense that the key points of the course have been adequately reviewed]

2. *On a sheet of paper, complete the four sentence stems you see written on the chalkboard. I will be collecting this as feedback to me about your experience in the course. Be as complete as possible.* [10–15 minutes; then collect what the students have written.]

3. *Now we're going to have a commencement exercise for our class. To commence means to "begin." So this exercise is the beginning of the rest of your lives. I invite you to come to the front of the room and talk to us from your heart and mind for a couple of minutes. Tell us what you've learned in this course; tell us what you want in your life; tell us what you know are the keys to your success; tell us anything else that you want us to know. When one person finishes, the next person can come right up. I'm just going to sit here and listen. Who would like to be first?* [10–25 minutes]

Approximate Time: 30–55 minutes

Instructor Notes:
1. Put the following four sentence stems on the chalkboard:
   1. Important goals and dreams in my life include . . .
   2. The success strategies I will use to achieve them include . . .
   3. Changes I would make in the course include . . .
   4. Most of all from this course I want to remember . . .

2. I recommend videotaping the commencement presentations. Students in your class will love watching themselves later, and the video is great to show at the beginning of future classes to show new students the amazing journey they are about to undertake. If appropriate, you can also use the video for recruiting new students to take your course.

3. You might want to mention that some students' Inner Critics or Inner Defenders will give them all sorts of reasons why they should not go to the front of the room and speak. That's why doing so is such a great boost to their self-esteem: They get to show their Inner Critics and Inner Defenders who is making the choices that matter.

EXERCISE 31-3: Appreciations

Purpose: To experience an avalanche of affirming thoughts that can boost the students' sense of self-worth.

Supplies and Setup: Journals; chime; students sitting in circles of 8 to 10. Write the words APPRECIATE, ADMIRE, RESPECT on the chalkboard or on an overhead transparency.

Directions:
1. *Open your journal to a clean page and write your name at the top of the page. Now pass your journal to the person on your right.* [1 minute]
2. *When you get your neighbor's journal, write a note on the blank page telling what you **appreciate, admire,** and **respect** about him or her. You'll have only two minutes, so get right to the heart of what you wish to say. When I ring the chime, sign your name and pass the journal to your right. Keep writing and passing until your journal comes back to you. Then read what people wrote to you.* [30–40 minutes]
3. *[Freewriting/Discussion] What was that experience like for you? What was it like to write appreciations to others? What was it like to read the appreciations written to you? How do you feel right now? What would it do for your success if you fully acknowledged all the aspects of yourself that others appreciate, admire, and respect? What is the life lesson here?* [10–20 minutes]

Approximate Time: 40–50 minutes

CHAPTER 9: Essay Topics

1. Most everyone would agree that they want to live a rich, personally fulfilling life—yet few people know what they mean by the idea, let alone how to create such a life. In an essay for *Success Magazine,* define what you consider to be a rich, personally fulfilling life and explain how you plan to create such a life.

2. In an essay to be given to your children (or grandchildren) on their twenty-first birthdays, present your philosophy of living a successful life. Be specific about what defines a successful life for you and how you plan to create it.

3. In an essay for the author of our textbook, *On Course,* explain what parts of the book you found most valuable and any that you found less valuable. Please send a copy of your essay to Skip Downing, c/o Houghton Mifflin Student Success Programs, 215 Park Avenue South, 11th Floor, New York, New York 10003.